Table of Contents

Copyright Page

From Campus to Corporate:

Navigating the Unknown

VERONICA OKOLA

An inspiring journey of leadership, resilience, and transformation—from university activism to navigating the complexities of corporate life, and ultimately building a platform for change.

"Success isn't just about personal achievement; it's about touching lives, creating opportunities, and paving the way for others to follow."

Acknowledgments

As I reflect on my journey, I am filled with gratitude for the incredible individuals who shaped, supported, and believed in me. This book is not just my story—it is a testament to their influence and unwavering encouragement.

I honor my late father, **Joram Lwambe Okola**, whose wisdom and values of leadership, resilience, and service continue to guide me. To my mother, **Sabina Okola**, your strength and belief in me have been my greatest source of courage. My brother, **Eric Okola**, and my siblings, thank you for your constant encouragement and love, which sustained me through every challenge.

To my mentors, **Professor Elyjoy Micheni**, **Irene Odongo**, and **Madam Anne Mucira**, your wisdom and guidance shaped my understanding of leadership, purpose, and professionalism. You taught me to rise above challenges and lead with integrity.

I am deeply grateful to my campaign team—**Kasmuel Oure, Adonija, James Odek, Marcy Keter, Michael Ratego**, and others—whose dedication and belief in our shared vision made success possible.

Finally, to the **Finsmart Hub community**, your resilience inspires my work every day. You are the reason this journey matters.

To all who supported me, mentored me, and walked this path with me—thank you. Your impact will forever be part of my story.

Chapter 1
My Journey

Welcome to my story a journey filled with challenges, triumphs, and invaluable lessons learned as a student leader at the Technical University of Kenya. As I reflect on my time there, I am reminded of the vibrant campus life, the late nights spent studying, and the exhilarating moments of leadership that shaped who I am today.

From the moment I stepped onto campus, I knew I wanted to make a difference. The Technical University of Kenya was not just an institution; it was a place where I could explore my passions, connect with diverse individuals, and advocate for my fellow students. But stepping into leadership came with its own set of challenges, especially as a woman in a field often dominated by male voices.

Throughout my journey, I faced obstacles that tested my resolve. There were moments of doubt, setbacks, and the pressure to prove myself. Yet, it was in these struggles that I discovered my strength and resilience. I learned to navigate the complex world of student governance, rally my peers, and champion causes that mattered to us all.

In this chapter, I will set the stage for my experiences, sharing how my journey began, the importance of student leadership in shaping our community, and the lessons that would guide me through both my time at university and beyond. Join me as

I delve into the vibrant, sometimes tumultuous, but ultimately rewarding experience of being a student leader at the Technical University of Kenya.

Importance of Student Leadership

Student leadership is vital in shaping both the student experience and the broader societal landscape. At institutions like the Technical University of Kenya, student leaders not only advocate for their peers but also lay the groundwork for future national leaders. Their experiences can profoundly influence Kenyan politics and policymaking, demonstrating the importance of youth engagement in shaping the nation's future.

Take James Orengo, for instance. While studying law at the University of Nairobi, he was elected chair of the Students' Organization of Nairobi University (SONU) from 1972 to 1973. During his tenure, Orengo was a vocal advocate for democratic rights and social justice, foreshadowing his future as a significant political figure. His leadership at SONU allowed him to hone skills in advocacy and mobilization, which he later applied to his work in Parliament. Orengo's commitment to constitutional reform has led to vital changes in Kenyan governance, including efforts to enhance human rights protections and promote transparency in public institutions.

Kipchumba Murkomen also exemplifies the impact of student leadership. As the chair of the Kenya Law School Students Society while pursuing his law degree, Murkomen was instrumental in fostering dialogue on legal reforms and student rights. His ability to advocate for his peers laid the foundation for his later success as a Senator and a prominent voice in national politics. Murkomen has played a crucial role in championing infrastructure development and enhancing the legal framework around education, thereby influencing policies that affect many Kenyans today.

Another remarkable figure is Gladys Wanga, who made history as the first woman to be elected Secretary-General at Kenyatta University. Her leadership journey began with initiatives aimed at empowering women on campus and addressing issues such as gender equality and access to education. Wanga's commitment to these causes has since translated into significant policy work as a Member of Parliament, where she has focused on improving women's rights and healthcare access. Her leadership not only inspired other young women but also reshaped discussions around women's representation in Kenyan politics.

These leaders illustrate the transformative power of student leadership. By addressing critical issues within their campuses, they foster a culture of advocacy that extends into their professional lives. Their experiences teach them how to navigate complex political landscapes, build coalitions, and champion policies that resonate with the needs of their constituents.

In the Kenyan context, the influence of student leaders like Orengo, Murkomen, and Wanga cannot be overstated. They have each contributed to shaping the current political climate, advocating for reforms that promote democratic governance and social justice. Their successes in the office highlight how the skills and insights gained during their student leadership experiences translate into meaningful change at the national level.

Student leadership serves as a vital incubator for future leaders, equipping them with the tools needed to effect change in society. As these individuals rise to national prominence, they carry with them the lessons learned during their university years—lessons that emphasize the importance of representation, advocacy, and community engagement. By empowering student leaders today, we lay a robust foundation for a more equitable and progressive Kenya tomorrow.

These leaders also serve as powerful examples of how student leadership can transform lives and influence national discourse. They have each contributed to shaping the current political climate, advocating for reforms that resonate with the needs of their constituents. Their journeys highlight the vital lessons learned in student leadership the importance of representation, advocacy, and community engagement.

As I reflect on my own journey, I recognize how my experiences at the Technical University of Kenya mirrored those of these remarkable leaders. Like Orengo, Murkomen, and Wanga, I faced challenges that tested my resolve and shaped my understanding of leadership. From navigating the complexities of student governance to addressing the needs of my peers, I learned the importance of resilience and advocacy.

I will share my own story of rising to student leadership amidst the unique challenges faced as a woman. I'll dive into the moments that shaped my journey, the victories that inspired me, and the lessons learned that continue to guide me today. Through my experiences, I hope to illustrate the profound impact that student leadership can have—not just on individuals, but on entire communities and the nation. Join me as I set the stage for my story, one that embodies the spirit of comradeship and its ability to drive change.

Chapter 2
Early Aspirations

This was my first time in Nairobi City, and the sights and sounds were a whirlwind of excitement and anxiety. Growing up in the serene countryside of Kanyikela Village in Ndhiwa, the hustle and bustle of the capital felt both thrilling and overwhelming. The tall buildings seemed to touch the sky, and the vibrant energy of the city pulsed all around me. Yet, amidst this vibrant chaos, I felt a nagging insecurity—my English wasn't as polished as I wished it to be. All I had was my confidence and a burning desire to make the most of this new chapter.

When I enrolled in the Bachelor of Commerce program at the Technical University of Kenya, I knew I was stepping into a world filled with opportunities. My initial experiences were a mix of wonder and trepidation. Navigating campus life in a city so vastly different from my village was daunting, but I was determined to rise to the occasion.

Soon after settling in, I was elected as my class representative. This role was my first taste of leadership, and while I may have stumbled with my words occasionally, I approached my responsibilities with a fierce commitment. I quickly learned that representing my classmates meant more than just passing along their concerns—it was about listening, empathizing, and advocating for them. Even with my limited language skills, I found ways to communicate and connect, proving that confidence could sometimes bridge the gaps left by inexperience.

It was during this time that I began to immerse myself in the political atmosphere on campus. My interactions with those vying for student leadership positions piqued my interest in the political landscape. It was invigorating to see my peers passionately debating ideas and visions for our student body. I wanted to be part of that energy, to be a voice for my classmates.

Then I met Brian Reeves Obare, who was running for Secretary General of the Students' Council. His charisma was magnetic, and his vision for a more inclusive student body resonated deeply with me. I was inspired by how he connected with students from various backgrounds, addressing their concerns with genuine empathy. It became clear to me that effective leadership was about more than just having the right words; it was about forging real connections.

Driven by my newfound passion, I volunteered for Brian's campaign team, known as "The Secretariat." This was my chance to dive headfirst into the world of student politics. I felt exhilarated as we organized rallies, crafted messages, and engaged with students across the campus. I learned the ropes of campaigning while also building friendships with others who shared my enthusiasm for change.

Participating in the campaign opened my eyes to the intricacies of leadership and the power of community. I remember the thrill of our first rally, where we gathered students in the quad to hear Brian speak. The energy in the air was electric, and despite my insecurities, I felt an overwhelming sense of belonging. I watched as Brian delivered his message with passion, connecting with students who were eager for change.

Throughout this experience, I realized that my confidence was my greatest asset. It allowed me to push through moments of doubt and engage with students, even when my English faltered. I learned to listen deeply, to empathize with my peers, and to advocate for their needs. Each interaction, each conversation, solidified my belief that leadership was about understanding and serving others.

The challenges we faced during the campaign—opposition from rival candidates and the pressures of public scrutiny—only strengthened my resolve. I witnessed how resilience and determination are crucial traits of effective leaders. Brian's ability to navigate these obstacles inspired me and deepened my commitment to the cause.

When Brian ultimately won the election, I felt a profound sense of pride in being part of that journey. It was a testament to the power of collective effort and the potential of student leadership to create meaningful change. This experience not only solidified my interest in politics but also shaped my understanding of what it means to be a leader.

As I look back, I realize that my early experiences as a "fresher" at the Technical University of Kenya laid the foundation for my future aspirations. They ignited a flame within me that would continue to burn brightly as I faced new challenges and opportunities in my journey ahead, proving that with confidence and determination, one can navigate even the most daunting of paths.

Background and Early Influences

Growing up in the picturesque Kanyikela Village in Ndhiwa, my upbringing was steeped in community values and resilience. The close-knit nature of my village taught me the importance of connection, collaboration, and supporting one another. My parents instilled in me a strong work ethic and a belief in the power of education as a pathway to a better life. These early lessons became the bedrock of my character and shaped my aspirations.

As I transitioned to the bustling environment of Nairobi and the Technical University of Kenya, I was acutely aware of how different my life had become. The urban landscape was a stark contrast to my rural roots, filled with new faces, ideas, and opportunities. It was during this transition that I began to encounter influential figures who would guide me on my journey into student politics.

In addition to Brian Reeves Obare, who played a significant role in igniting my interest in leadership, I was fortunate to meet Ricky Brian Ambuli, who was vying for the presidential position of the Students' Council. Ricky's charisma and determination were infectious. His vision for a united and empowered student body resonated with me, and I was drawn to his inclusive approach to leadership. Ricky became not just a mentor but also a friend who encouraged me to believe in my potential. He often reminded me that leadership is about serving others and listening to their needs—a lesson that would stick with me throughout my journey.

My classmates also had a profound influence on my early aspirations. Many of them were passionate, driven individuals who believed in the power of student leadership to effect change. Their support was invaluable. They often encouraged me to voice my ideas, reminding me that my unique perspective was essential to the conversation. This camaraderie fostered a sense of belonging and motivated me to step outside my comfort zone.

In our study groups, discussions often veered into the political realm, analyzing current events and debating the issues affecting our campus and country. These conversations ignited my passion for politics and advocacy. I began to see how the principles we learned in class applied to real-world situations, and I felt a growing responsibility to engage with these issues beyond the classroom.

Moreover, the mentorship I received from my professors further shaped my political outlook. They encouraged critical thinking and emphasized the importance of civic engagement. Their insights into the political landscape of Kenya inspired me to consider how I could contribute to positive change, not just as a student but as a future leader.

The combination of these influences created a fertile ground for my aspirations to grow. The encouragement from Ricky, the support from my classmates, and the guidance from my professors all played a crucial role in shaping my understanding of leadership. They taught me that being a leader is not just about authority; it's about empathy, service, and the willingness to stand up for what is right.

As I embarked on my journey into student politics, I carried these lessons with me. The belief that I could make a difference, combined with the support of those around me, fueled my determination to advocate for my peers and navigate the complexities of leadership. These early influences were instrumental in molding my aspirations and preparing me for the challenges that lay ahead.

Initial Interest in Leadership

My interest in leadership can be traced back to my childhood, where the seeds of political awareness were sown early. At the age of 11, I watched my father, the late Joram Okola, immerse himself in local politics. His involvement was not just a pastime; it was a calling that led him to become part of the Luo Council of Elders. He often brought home stories of political discussions and decisions that shaped our community. The importance of leadership and representation was a frequent topic at our dinner table, where debates flowed freely.

My father recognized my curiosity and actively nurtured it. He would buy newspapers, carefully selecting the political columns and then encouraging me to read them. I still remember the thrill of those evenings spent poring over the latest news. Afterward, he would ask me to narrate what I had learned, prompting me to articulate my thoughts and develop my understanding of current events. This practice not only sharpened my comprehension skills but also instilled in me a sense of responsibility to engage with the world around me.

During that formative period, I found myself particularly inspired by Martha Karua, a formidable political figure known for her unwavering courage and determination. I admired her fierce advocacy for justice and her relentless pursuit of equality. To me, she embodied the essence of strength, and I often referred to her as "Justina Valor," a name that symbolized her bravery and tenacity. She was making headlines, not just for her political achievements but for her boldness in challenging the status quo. Martha became a role model; someone I aspired to emulate in my own journey.

As I transitioned into my teenage years, the lessons from my father and the examples set by leaders like Martha fueled my burgeoning interest in leadership and politics. I began to understand that leadership was not merely about holding a position; it was about advocating for others, understanding their needs, and being a voice for the voiceless. My father's guidance and the political discussions we shared deepened my appreciation for the complexities of governance and the power of active citizenship.

When I arrived at the Technical University of Kenya, this early foundation took on new significance. Surrounded by peers who shared my passion for change, I felt inspired to channel my interests into action. The campaign rallies, debates, and discussions on campus were a natural extension of the conversations I had once shared with my father. The energy and vibrancy of student politics resonated with me, and I knew I wanted to be part of it.

With each passing day, I drew upon the lessons of resilience, courage, and empathy that I had learned from my father and admired in leaders like Martha Karua. They served as reminders that effective leadership is about serving others, embracing challenges, and standing firm in one's beliefs. As I began to explore opportunities for involvement on campus, I felt a growing sense of purpose. The initial interest that had sparked during my childhood was now blossoming into a commitment to advocate for my peers and champion the causes that mattered most to us.

Armed with the wisdom of my upbringing and the inspiration from the leaders I admired, I was ready to embark on my journey into student leadership—eager to transform my early aspirations into meaningful action and to make my mark in a world that was as complex as it was full of promise.

Challenges Faced in School

Transitioning from the Village to the vibrant, fast-paced environment of the Technical University of Kenya was not without its challenges. While I was excited to embrace new experiences and opportunities, I quickly realized that navigating university life would test my resilience in ways I had never anticipated.

One of the most significant hurdles was the academic pressure. The shift to a more rigorous educational system meant that I had to adapt quickly. Many of my peers had come from well-resourced backgrounds, with access to private schools and extensive tutoring. In contrast, I found myself grappling with concepts that felt overwhelming at times. Despite my determination, there were moments when self-doubt crept in, and I questioned whether I belonged to such an esteemed institution. However, I leaned on the support of my classmates, who became my study partners and friends, reminding me that we were all in this together.

Another challenge stemmed from my background and the language barrier. Though I had grown up reading newspapers and engaging in political discussions, speaking English fluently in academic settings was daunting. My confidence would waver during presentations or group discussions, and I often felt the weight of judgment from peers. To overcome this, I sought out opportunities to practice speaking—whether through participating in class discussions or joining clubs where I could refine my communication skills. Each small victory bolstered my confidence and helped me realize that growth often comes from stepping outside one's comfort zone.

Moreover, as a woman aspiring to take on leadership roles, I encountered societal expectations that sometimes clashed with my ambitions. There were instances where my opinions were overshadowed in discussions dominated by louder voices. It was disheartening to witness the subtle biases that often went unnoticed by others. However, these experiences ignited a fire within me. I became determined not only to assert my own voice but to uplift those around me who might also be marginalized. I sought mentorship and guidance from female leaders in student governance, learning from their journeys and strategies for overcoming such barriers.

Balancing academics and extracurricular activities were another significant challenge. As I became more involved in student politics and advocacy, I struggled to maintain my class attendance. Late nights spent organizing events or attending meetings often left me exhausted, and I found it difficult to juggle both responsibilities effectively. There were times when I felt overwhelmed, questioning whether I could continue to pursue my passions while keeping my grades up. To navigate this, I learned the importance of time management and prioritization. I developed a schedule that allowed me to allocate time for studying while also fulfilling my commitments to the student council and my peers.

Lastly, the emotional toll of facing challenges in a new environment sometimes felt isolated. There were moments when I missed the familiarity of my village—the warmth of my community and the unwavering support of my family. In those times, I sought solace in the friendships I had forged at university. My classmate Zippy Onyango became my second family, offering encouragement and understanding during moments of self-doubt. Together, we navigated the ups and downs of university life, celebrating each other's victories and providing a shoulder to lean on when needed.

Ultimately, these challenges were invaluable teachers. They not only shaped my character but also reinforced my commitment to leadership. I learned that true resilience lies in facing adversity head-on and that every obstacle can be an opportunity for growth. Through these experiences, I developed a deeper understanding of the complexities of leadership and the importance of advocating for oneself and others.

As I moved forward in my journey, I carried these lessons with me, knowing that each challenge I faced was not just a setback but a steppingstone toward becoming the leader I aspired to be.

Chapter 3
The Rise to Leadership

The moment I was elected as my class representative, a new chapter in my life began, one that would be filled with ambition, determination, and more than a few hurdles. It wasn't just a title or a stepping stone; it was the first real test of my ability to lead, to represent, and to fight for the interests of my classmates. At the time, I didn't know just how far this path would take me, but I was eager to find out.

The First Step Class Representative

Becoming a class representative came with its own set of challenges. It wasn't a glamorous role, but it was essential. It required late-night discussions, problem-solving meetings, and most importantly, listening. Listening to the concerns of my classmates—whether it was about overcrowded lecture halls, outdated materials, or unfair exam schedules—became my daily reality. It was in this role that I first learned the art of advocacy. I didn't have all the answers, and I didn't always know how to approach the administration, but I knew how to listen and how to care. Sometimes, that's what my classmates needed most.

In this role, I also learned how to navigate the often chaotic landscape of university bureaucracy. Getting anything done required persistence and patience, two qualities that I hadn't fully mastered yet but would come to develop over time. The more I worked through the challenges, the more I felt an emerging sense of purpose—a deeper understanding that leadership was more than a title. It was a responsibility, a calling. This feeling of purpose drove me to aim higher.

The Setback Running for College of Business Representative

With the confidence I'd built as a class representative, I decided it was time to step up my game. The position of College of Business representative seemed like the perfect opportunity to make a bigger impact, not just for my classmates but for students across the entire college. So, I threw my hat into the ring.

I was determined. I rallied my friends, created a solid campaign strategy, and spent hours talking to students, gathering support, and crafting a message that resonated. I thought I had it in the bag. But then came election day, and everything changed.

I LOST.

The sting of that defeat was sharper than I'd expected. I'd put everything into that campaign, and to see it fall short was more than disappointing—it was a blow to my confidence. For a moment, I questioned everything. Was I cut out for this? Had I been too ambitious too soon? The voices of doubt crept in, louder than ever.

But in those moments of reflection, I realized something important leadership is not defined by a single win or loss. It's defined by resilience. I remembered the words of my mentor, Brian Reeves Obare, who once told me, **"A true leader is one who can get back up after falling.**

Losing doesn't mean you're not a leader; it just means there's more to learn." That loss became my turning point. Instead of retreating, I decided to use it as fuel. If anything, it strengthened my resolve.

A Comeback Winning as Congress Lady

The next election cycle, I decided to aim for a different position Congress Lady. It was a role that would allow me to represent an even broader constituency of students across the university, giving me the chance to build a stronger foundation for future leadership. But this time, I was wiser. I approached this campaign with a new mindset. I wasn't just running to win; I was running to serve, to connect, and to learn.

The campaign was intense, but I was ready. I had learned from my mistakes. I built stronger alliances, refined my messaging, and connected with students on a more personal level. I didn't just want their vote; I wanted to understand their struggles, their hopes, and their vision for what student leadership could achieve.

When the election results came in, I had won. The victory was sweet, not just because it was a win, but because it represented redemption. It was proof that persistence and resilience could pay off. Winning as Congress Lady gave me a renewed sense of confidence and purpose. I had regained my footing and was ready to take on the challenges ahead.

The Big Leap Vice President of the Student Council

After serving as Congress Lady, my vision for what I could accomplish began to grow. I saw the potential to make real change, not just within the confines of my college, but across the entire student body. And that's when I made the bold decision to run for Vice President of the Student Council.

This was a position that came with a lot more scrutiny, more responsibility, and more pressure. The stakes were higher, and the race was fierce. But I knew I was ready. I had faced defeat, I had faced victory, and I had learned from both. I was no longer the wide-eyed student leader who doubted her place at the table. I had earned my spot, and I was ready to claim it.

The campaign for Vice President was grueling. It required not just strategy but stamina. Long nights, back-to-back meetings, and constant rallies became my new normal. My competitors were formidable, but I didn't let that shake me. I knew what I stood for. I knew why I was running. I had built a solid team around me—friends and supporters who believed in my vision and who had been with me since my first days as a class representative.

One of the most memorable moments from that campaign was the final debate. I stood on stage, facing off against the other candidates, each one determined to win. The room was packed, and the energy was palpable. When it was my turn to speak,

I felt a wave of calm wash over me. I spoke from the heart. I talked about my journey, my belief in student leadership, and my vision for a more inclusive, transparent, and empowered student council. And when I finished, the applause was deafening.

Election day came, and the tension was thick in the air. I remember sitting with my team, nervously waiting for the results. When my name was called, declaring me the new Vice President of the Student Council, it felt surreal. I had done it. I had climbed the ladder from class representative to the second-highest position in student governance. It was the culmination of years of hard work, failures, lessons, and victories.

Reflections on Leadership

Looking back on my journey, I realized that each step—whether it was a victory or a defeat—taught me something valuable about leadership. It's not about the title or the accolades; it's about the resilience, the passion, and the commitment to serve others. Losing the College of Business election was one of the best things that ever happened to me because it taught me to be humble, to work harder, and to never take success for granted.

Winning as Vice President wasn't just about personal achievement; it was about realizing the power of student leadership to effect real change. I had gone from representing a single class to representing an entire university. And through it all, I learned that leadership is about lifting others up, not just yourself.

As I moved forward in my role as Vice President, I carried with me all the lessons I'd learned along the way—the importance of listening, the necessity of resilience, and the power of believing in your vision, even when the odds seem stacked against you. My rise to leadership was not a straight line, but it was a journey that shaped me into the leader I aspired to be, and one that I hoped would inspire others to follow their own path, no matter the challenges they might face.

Campaigning and Election Process A Battle of Loyalties and Survival

Running for Vice President of the Student Council was unlike any other campaign I had ever undertaken. It wasn't just about strategy, charisma, or a good track record—it was a battlefield, where alliances could make or break your chances. My decision to team up with the "House of Gema" over my own community, the "House of Tukelsa," made this campaign even more chaotic, and more personal.

The House of Gema and the Tribal Clashes

Kenya's university politics, much like national politics, are steeped in tribal affiliations. At my university, this manifested in student elections in a big way. The "House of Gema," a powerful student faction, primarily represented the Kikuyu, Kamba, and Ameru students, communities from the central and eastern regions of Kenya. On the other hand, the "House of Tukelsa" represented my own people, the Luo, Luhya tribes. Typically, in such elections, candidates from each tribal group would align with their respective factions to maximize support. That's what made my choice so controversial.

Teaming up with the "House of Gema" wasn't easy. I knew it would mean going against the grain, against the expected path of seeking support from my own people. In theory, running with the "House of Tukelsa" should have offered me ready backing—after all, I was one of their own. But politics, even in university, is rarely that simple.

The "House of Tukelsa" had their preferred candidates, and I wasn't one of them. I had seen enough betrayals in previous elections to know that loyalty wasn't guaranteed just because we shared a tribe. So I took a gamble. I aligned myself with the "House of Gema," a move that made many of my friends and supporters within the Luo community question my loyalty. But I wasn't running for tribal endorsement. I was running for leadership, for everyone. My decision cost me significant support, and the whispers of betrayal spread quickly.

The Costly Game of Delegate Politics

Elections at my university weren't just about popularity or rhetoric. The delegate voting system was a game-changer—and an expensive one at that. Delegates were elected representatives from various faculties, and they were the ultimate decision-makers in the student council elections. This meant that instead of convincing thousands of students directly, I had to win over these elusive delegates. And that was no easy task.

Rumor had it that many delegates could be "bought" with cash, gifts, or even promises of future favors. The stakes were high, and candidates with deep pockets had the upper hand. Unfortunately, I didn't have deep pockets. The money flowing in some campaigns was staggering—posters, rallies, "handshakes" to delegates—all of it required a budget I couldn't dream of. My opponents, many of whom had the backing of well-off families or local politicians, seemed to have limitless resources. In contrast, I was relying on loyalty and the belief that some people would back me not because I could pay them, but because they believed in me.

And that's where things got tricky.

The Elusiveness of Delegates

The delegates, in many ways, held all the power. They were the kingmakers, and they knew it. Convincing them to support me wasn't just about presenting a solid vision or a heartfelt speech. It was about the politics behind closed doors—the alliances they had already formed; the promises they had already received. I'd call them for meetings, only for them to show up late or not at all. They became masters of the elusive art of making you chase them. Some would promise their votes, smile, shake your hand, but you could never be sure. The next day, they'd be at a rally for one of your competitors.

At one point, I felt like I was running in circles, chasing ghosts. Every time I thought I had secured a delegate's support, I'd hear rumors of them having been "convinced" by someone else. The uncertainty was suffocating. In those moments, I questioned whether this was all worth it. Was I really cut out for this level of political maneuvering?

The Betrayals

The hardest part of the campaign wasn't the pressure or the competition—it was the betrayals. The very people I had thought would stand by me, those who had promised loyalty, turned their backs when I needed them most. Some from my own community openly campaigned against me. It stung. These were people I had grown up with, shared classes with, friends who I thought would support me simply because we had history. But in politics, even history can be rewritten.

I remember vividly one of my closest allies from the Luo community, someone who had initially promised to rally support for me. We had been friends since first year. I counted on his influence among the "House of Tukelsa" to sway a few votes my way, even after my controversial alignment with the "House of Gema." But as the days went by, I started hearing whispers—he was quietly rallying behind my opponent. When I confronted him, his excuses were vague, something about "doing what's best for the community." It felt like a knife in the back.

That betrayal hit hard. It wasn't just about the votes—I could handle losing. It was the feeling of being abandoned by those I thought would be with me through thick and thin. But even then, I knew I couldn't afford to dwell on it. I had a campaign to run, and time was running out.

Overcoming the Odds

Despite the chaos, the tribal politics, and the betrayals, there were moments of hope. There were students who saw beyond tribal lines, who believed in what I stood for. My campaign wasn't flashy. I didn't have money to throw lavish events or buy loyalty, but I had a message that resonated with those who believed in a more inclusive student leadership. I wasn't running to divide; I was running to unite.

My rallies weren't the biggest, but they were passionate. I focused on showing students that I wasn't just another candidate vying for power. I was there to represent them—all of them—regardless of where they came from. Slowly but surely, word began to spread. Some delegates who had been elusive started showing interest, if only out of curiosity at first. They attended my rallies, asked questions, and over time, some began to genuinely support me.

One of the most memorable moments came just days before the election. I had been struggling to secure the votes of a group of delegates from the School of Health and sciences. They were known to be tough to win over, and they had been leaning heavily towards my main opponent. But after one particularly heated debate, where I had spoken from the heart about my vision for student leadership, something shifted. Several of them approached me afterward, offering their support. It was a small victory, but it meant the world to me.

Victory, Against All Odds

Election day arrived, and the tension was thick in the air. Delegates filed into the voting hall, their faces betraying nothing of their intentions. I had done everything I could. I had fought through tribal divisions, through betrayals, through a lack of resources. All that was left was to wait.

When the results were finally announced, I could hardly believe it—I had won. By a wide margin, yes, I had done it. The delegates had chosen me, despite everything stacked against me. The room erupted in cheers, and as I stood there, I felt a wave of emotion wash over me. The journey had been grueling, but the victory was all the sweeter because of it.

Reflections on the Campaign

Looking back, I realize that the chaos of that campaign taught me some of the most valuable lessons about leadership. It taught me that true leadership isn't about the easiest path, but about the one that challenges you, that tests your resilience and forces you to stand by your principles. I learned that loyalty is rare but invaluable when you find it. And most importantly, I learned that even in the murky waters of university politics, where tribal lines run deep and money often speaks louder than words, there is always space for integrity.

This campaign was more than just an election—it was a test of character. And through it all, I came out stronger, more determined, and ready to lead.

Bottom of Form

Support Systems and Mentorship Building My Inner Circle

Behind every successful campaign, every victory, and every moment of triumph is an often overlooked but crucial element—the people who stand with you through the chaos. As I prepared to navigate the most daunting election of my university life, I quickly learned that the strength of your support system could be the difference between breaking through or breaking down. For me, these were not just mentors or friends, they were lifelines, guiding me when I stumbled and pushing me when I doubted myself.

The Silent Architect Professor Elyjoy Micheni's Wisdom

Every great leader has someone in the shadows—a figure who doesn't stand in the spotlight but who plays a pivotal role in shaping their journey. For me, that person was Professor Elyjoy Micheni, the then Director of the School of Business. I had come across her in one of the school forums, and her presence was undeniable—wise, calm, and fiercely intelligent. I knew immediately that she was someone I needed in my corner.

When I first told her about my decision to run for Vice President, she didn't offer immediate praise or encouragement. Instead, she looked at me with her calm yet piercing gaze and asked, "Why do you want this?" It wasn't a simple question, and it quickly became clear she wasn't looking for a superficial answer. I tried to articulate my passion for student leadership and my desire to create a more inclusive environment. She listened patiently, but remained silent.

After what felt like an eternity, she finally said, "Good. But you'll need more than passion. You need a strategy. Do you have one?"

That moment marked the beginning of a mentorship that would shape not just my campaign, but my entire understanding of leadership. Professor Micheni wasn't the kind of mentor who handed you answers. When I stumbled, she pointed it out with brutal honesty. When I succeeded, she didn't shower me with praise. Instead, she would say, "What's the next step?"

During one particularly exhausting week, when the delegates seemed unreachable and I was drained both mentally and physically, I confided in her, "I don't think I can do this anymore."

Her response was as sharp as ever "You're tired. That's okay. But you'll keep going. Leadership isn't about doing it when it's easy. It's about doing it when you're convinced you'll fail, and still pushing through."

Her words stayed with me, driving me forward when I felt like giving up.

The Pillars of Strength My Team

If Professor Micheni was the silent architect of my leadership journey, my campaign team was the engine that kept everything moving. This team was not just made up of close friends—they were my warriors, each bringing a unique strength to the table.

First, there was Kasmuel Oure, a friend and the voice of reason when things got chaotic. He was the strategist—the one who could take a jumble of ideas and turn them into a cohesive plan. When I was overwhelmed by the demands of delegate meetings, endless debates, and rally planning, Kasmuel would sit me down, break everything into manageable pieces, and remind me that I didn't have to solve everything at once.

Then there was Adonija, the energizer. His job was to hype the crowd and rally the troops. If I was the brain of the campaign, Adonija was its heart. His infectious enthusiasm drew people in, and even in the bleakest moments, he was there, pushing us forward with his unwavering belief that we were going to win. He would stay up late, tirelessly making calls and organizing volunteers. Even when the odds seemed stacked against us, Adonija's confidence never wavered.

James Odek, although quiet and reserved, was perhaps one of the most impactful members of my team. He had been part of the university's debate team and wasn't one for flash or spectacle. But when James spoke, his words carried weight. He was my moral compass. When I felt the temptation to cut corners or engage in the dirty tactics some of my opponents excelled at, it was James who kept me grounded. He reminded me that we were running for something bigger than just a position. We were fighting for integrity.

And finally, there was Marcy Keter. Marcy was our logistics guru—the person who made sure that everything ran smoothly. Whether it was organizing meetings, securing venues, or handling the thousands of little details that kept the campaign on track, Marcy was always a step ahead, ensuring that nothing was left to chance.

Moments of Doubt

Despite the incredible support from Professor Micheni and my team, there were moments when even the best guidance and most loyal friends couldn't shield me from self-doubt. One of the toughest moments came when a key delegate—someone I had been relying on for support—suddenly switched sides. It was a crushing blow.

When I found out, I was in the middle of a team meeting. The news hit me hard, and for a moment, I couldn't speak. Without that delegate, our chances seemed grim. The room fell silent as everyone realized what had just happened. Adonija, ever the optimist, tried to say something reassuring, but I needed space to process the setback. I stepped outside, my mind racing, wondering if I had made the right choices, or if I should have fought harder to secure my own backyard.

As I sat on a bench, staring at the campus lawns, I felt someone sit beside me. It was James. He didn't say anything at first, just sat there quietly. After a long pause, he finally spoke "You're not going to win every battle. But that doesn't mean you're losing the war."

His words, though simple, were exactly what I needed to hear. I wasn't going to win every delegate, but that didn't mean I wasn't on the right path. Leadership isn't about winning every fight—it's about staying true to your values, even when the easier option is staring you in the face.

Strength in Belief

As the campaign progressed, I started to realize that what I lacked in financial backing or political clout, I more than made up for in something far more valuable—belief. The belief that Professor Micheni had instilled in me, and the unwavering faith of my team, had built something greater than a campaign. Together, we had built a movement.

I may not have had the luxury of buying votes, but I had something much more powerful the genuine support of students who believed in my vision. And that was my biggest strength.

Chapter 4
The Struggles of Leadership

Stepping into leadership, especially in a university setting, can feel exhilarating at first. You're eager to make a difference, riding on the momentum of your campaign promises, believing you're going to be the one to change everything. But as I quickly learned, leadership is as much about challenges and setbacks as it is about progress. In Kenya's university context, where cultural complexities and power dynamics are woven into the fabric of student politics, the realities of leadership hit even harder.

Balancing Diverse Expectations

The first challenge was learning to manage the diverse expectations of the students who had elected me. In a student council role, especially as Vice President, you're a mediator for so many different groups and communities. Each of these groups has its own agenda, needs, and grievances. There were the academically-focused students who demanded improved resources and study environments, the athletes who needed better funding for their teams, and the social activists pushing for more progressive policies.

Many students expected immediate action, hoping that my victory would bring instant solutions. But the hard truth was that the bureaucracy within the university administration made even minor changes a drawn-out process. I was met with red tape, formalities, and approvals that took weeks, sometimes months. My attempts to make changes were often met with procedural obstacles, frustrating students who thought I simply wasn't trying hard enough.

In one instance, we had lobbied for extended library hours, a simple enough request that students had been pushing for years. After countless meetings and discussions, the administration agreed to a pilot program. But the extended hours only lasted for a week before they were rolled back due to budget constraints. Students felt betrayed, and I was caught in the middle, trying to explain that it wasn't lack of effort but rather a lack of resources. This early experience showed me that even with the best intentions, a leader's hands can be tied by limitations outside their control.

Navigating Tribal Politics and Allegiances

The complexities of tribal affiliations in Kenya, though often unspoken, were never far from the surface. This reality became painfully clear as I took on a leadership role where students from every corner of the country looked to me as their representative. During the campaign, I had aligned myself with the House of Gema, a coalition representing students from central Kenya. While this strategic alliance had helped me secure votes, it also placed me at odds with the House of Tukelsa, which represented my own Luo community and other communities from my region.

Some students saw me as a bridge between groups, while others viewed me as a betrayer of my roots. I found myself in a delicate balancing act, trying to maintain unity and neutrality. Yet there were times when the divisions were stark and unavoidable. In some meetings, I was openly questioned about why I had chosen one side over the other, as though my leadership was only valid if I had the full support of my own tribe. This was one of the toughest aspects of student politics—the constant reminder that, to some, I would always be defined first by my ethnicity rather than my actions or intentions.

Financial Challenges and Limited Resources

Leadership on a Kenyan campus is not just about vision and resilience; it's also about dealing with harsh financial realities. As a leader, students expected me to organize events, offer support for those in need, and sometimes even step in to help fund activities that the council's budget could not cover. I quickly realized that the expectations students had of their leaders often extended beyond my actual capacity.

The student council's budget was limited and strictly regulated, meaning we often had to prioritize only the most essential needs. Yet this was a far cry from what students envisioned. They wanted events, improvements in their daily lives, and even financial assistance, all of which were difficult to provide without the necessary funds. To some, this lack of visible impact was disappointing, but I learned that transparency and honesty went a long way. If I couldn't deliver on something, I'd tell them why, rather than make empty promises that would only lead to frustration later on.

Balancing Academics with Responsibilities

Amid all these responsibilities, I was still a student, juggling lectures, assignments, and exams just like everyone else. University leadership often makes balancing academics and leadership nearly impossible, and Kenya's system is no exception. The sheer amount of time that meetings, planning, and interactions took meant that I was constantly struggling to keep up with my coursework. Some professors understood the pressures of leadership, but others saw it as an excuse. I vividly remember failing an important test simply because I'd been too overwhelmed by council work to study adequately.

I found myself studying late into the night or early in the morning to catch up, squeezing in moments to work on assignments between meetings. There were times when the pressure felt unbearable, when I wondered if I had bitten off more than I could chew. Yet, in some ways, the struggles made me stronger, forcing me to learn time management and prioritize my commitments with precision.

Handling Backlash and Criticism

No leader can escape criticism, and in the high-stakes world of student politics, it often comes from every direction. Some students felt I was not doing enough; others were critical of the alliances I had formed. Then there were those who simply didn't like that I had won. On social media, I became the target of harsh comments and personal attacks. Every decision I made was scrutinized, dissected, and sometimes even misrepresented.

One of the hardest parts of leadership is learning not to take things personally. I discovered that not every criticism required a response, and that sometimes silence was the best answer. But that didn't mean it was easy. Reading comments that questioned my intentions or accused me of favoritism was difficult, especially when I knew how hard I was working to make a difference. Over time, I learned to listen carefully to constructive criticism and block out the noise that was only there to distract me.

Finding My Resilience

The struggles of leadership are unrelenting, but they also bring about growth and self-awareness. I was forced to confront my weaknesses, to ask for help when I needed it, and to make decisions that I knew would not please everyone. It was a humbling experience, one that taught me the value of resilience and the strength of character required to stand firm in the face of challenges.

Ultimately, the struggles didn't diminish my passion for leadership—they deepened it. Every setback, every criticism, every sleepless night was a step toward becoming a stronger, more determined leader. I learned that true leadership isn't about avoiding struggles; it's about facing them with courage and integrity.

Challenges Faced as a Woman Leader

Leadership as a woman within a Kenyan university context presented layers of complexity. While I had anticipated that my path wouldn't be straightforward, I wasn't fully prepared for the subtle and sometimes blatant ways my gender would be questioned and scrutinized. Being a woman leader meant constantly proving my competence, not just once but over and over, as if each success was forgotten the moment it was achieved.

In meetings, I would notice how my male counterparts often received more acknowledgment for the same ideas I had raised minutes before. I became accustomed to the subtle glances, the sideways looks, the subtle hesitations when I would speak. Many students seemed to have this unspoken assumption that a woman's role, even in leadership, was to be accommodating and less assertive. But I wasn't about to compromise my voice or my vision just to fit into a box others had built for me.

One particularly frustrating incident occurred during a council meeting when a major decision was on the line. We were discussing a controversial proposal involving increased funding for student wellness programs. When I spoke up in favor of it, some council members accused me of being too "emotionally invested" in the issue. Yet when a male colleague supported the proposal minutes later, his words were met with agreement and serious consideration. It was a moment that stung deeply, not only because of the disregard but because I knew that being dismissed on the basis of gender was something many female leaders before me had faced and something many would continue to encounter.

But rather than let it discourage me, I used these experiences to strengthen my resolve. I learned to speak with clarity, to back up my positions with data and logic so irrefutable that no one could dismiss it. Over time, I also found unexpected allies, both men and women who saw the value in my perspective and appreciated the balance I brought to the council. In that way, the challenges I faced as a woman leader shaped me, teaching me that leadership requires resilience and a belief in oneself that is unwavering, even when others don't yet see your potential.

Balancing Studies and Leadership Roles

Balancing my responsibilities as Vice President with my academic work turned out to be one of the most intense juggling acts I'd ever attempted. Between council meetings, student welfare events, endless emails, and ongoing conflict resolution tasks, I barely had time left to breathe, let alone focus on my coursework. The pressure to perform well academically was immense. After all, as a student leader, I was expected to model success in every area of university life.

In the beginning, I tried to fit everything into a strict schedule, determined to keep both my grades and my leadership duties on track. But leadership is unpredictable, and it wasn't long before my well-laid plans began to crumble under the demands of reality. There were nights when I'd sit in my dorm room with a thick textbook open in front of me, trying to study while my phone buzzed constantly with notifications from my team. Messages from students seeking assistance, updates on council matters, and calls from delegates needed my immediate attention, leaving me unable to fully focus on either my studies or my leadership role.

It was particularly challenging during exam season. One week, I had three exams scheduled back-to-back while also organizing a crucial event on campus. The event required multiple meetings with the administration and extensive logistical planning. I found myself studying in short bursts between meetings, frantically trying to cram information at odd hours. Inevitably, my grades began to show the strain, and I felt a profound guilt that I was letting down my professors, my team, and even myself.

Realizing I couldn't continue on this path, I reached out to a professor who had been supportive in the past, Professor Elyjoy Micheni, who had become a mentor of sorts. She helped me see that it wasn't weakness to ask for help or to delegate. With her encouragement, I made changes to my approach, setting stricter boundaries for my time and trusting my team to take on more responsibilities. I still struggled to balance it all, but I was learning the art of prioritization. Most importantly, I learned that leadership isn't about doing everything alone; it's about knowing when to ask for help and empowering those around you to lead alongside you.

Conflict Resolution and Team Dynamics

One of the most demanding parts of being in a leadership position was managing the dynamics within my team and handling the inevitable conflicts that would arise. Our team, composed of students from diverse backgrounds and different faculties, often had varying perspectives on how to tackle issues. I quickly learned that conflict was an unavoidable part of working with people and that resolving these conflicts was essential to maintaining unity and progress.

The most memorable conflict emerged around a high-stakes event we were planning to address students' mental health. Some team members felt strongly that we should partner with external mental health organizations, while others thought this would shift the focus away from the university and possibly divert funding. Tensions flared during our meetings, with some of the team accusing others of disregarding the students' voices. Our normally cohesive team was suddenly divided, and as Vice President, I was thrust into the role of mediator.

At first, I attempted to smooth things over by encouraging everyone to compromise, but this only led to more frustration. Realizing my approach wasn't working, I decided to listen more deeply to each side, meeting individually with team members to understand their concerns. One by one, I gathered their input, allowing them to express their frustrations and their ideas without fear of judgment. I took their perspectives into consideration and crafted a revised plan that acknowledged both sides, balancing the need for external support with a strong student-centered focus.

Once I presented this plan to the team, the atmosphere shifted. While not everyone was entirely satisfied, they appreciated that their voices had been heard and that we were moving forward as a unified team. It was a powerful reminder of the importance of communication, patience, and empathy in leadership.

Conflict resolution wasn't about forcing everyone to agree but rather about creating a space where differing views could coexist and even strengthen our shared goals.

Through each of these challenges, I learned that leadership is as much about character and empathy as it is about strategy and vision. The ability to stay true to my values, to push through the difficult times, and to bring people together despite our differences became the foundation of my growth as a leader.

Chapter 5
Moments of Triumph

Leadership is often defined by its challenges, but it's the triumphs—those rare, shining moments that make it all worthwhile—that remind us why we started in the first place. The journey to reach these moments was anything but easy. Every victory was built on a foundation of persistence, strategy, and support from those who stood by me. These were the milestones that made every sleepless night, every compromise, every sacrifice, worth it.

Victory as Vice President

The day of the election results will always remain etched in my memory as one of the most surreal experiences of my life. Standing among my team, my heart pounded with the suspense that hung in the air, thick and nearly tangible. The election had been intense, full of heated debates, long nights, and nail-biting campaign moments, but it all came down to this one announcement. I remember clutching the hands of those around me, including my team's loyal members like Kasmuel Oure, Adonija, James Odek, and Marcy Keter. We were no longer just colleagues—we had become family.

When my name was finally called, the room erupted. Cheers, applause, and the sound of my own heartbeat filled my ears, yet all I could feel was this overwhelming sense of gratitude. I had achieved something monumental, not just for myself, but for everyone who believed in me. I saw the pride on my team's faces, and in that moment, I knew that our work was only just beginning. I was no longer just another student on campus; I was now a representative, a voice for the students, and I was determined to live up to their trust.

Launching the Student Wellness Program

One of the most memorable projects during my term as Vice President was launching the Student Wellness Program. Mental health had been a recurring concern across campus, with students struggling silently, many unsure where to turn for support. This was more than just a program to me—it was a chance to create something lasting, a resource for students to feel seen, supported, and understood.

The planning stages were demanding. Securing funding and organizing partnerships with mental health organizations was a constant negotiation, but the moment we held the program's launch event, I felt an immense sense of accomplishment. Students attended in droves, many of whom shared how they had been waiting for an initiative like this. Seeing their gratitude made every meeting, every sleepless night, and every battle for budget approval worth it. More importantly, it felt like we were creating a culture of openness and support, helping students recognize that they were not alone in their struggles.

Creating the First Student-Led Campus Business Incubator

Our university had long attracted students with entrepreneurial ambitions, but the resources to turn these ambitions into reality were limited. My team and I set out to change this by creating a student-led business incubator that would offer workshops, networking events, and mentorship programs to aspiring entrepreneurs. It was ambitious and a bit unprecedented, but I was determined to see it through.

The process was not easy—every department seemed to have a different requirement, every form seemed to require another signature, and we had to convince university stakeholders that students could indeed take the lead on this initiative. But step by step, we made progress. Eventually, we secured a small office space on campus, funded by donations and small grants, where students could meet, plan, and grow their business ideas.

The grand opening was one of my proudest moments. As I cut the ribbon, surrounded by students buzzing with excitement, I saw the impact we were creating. This wasn't just a campus initiative; it was a launchpad for futures, a place where students could turn dreams into viable plans. Knowing that we had created something tangible, something that would continue to support students long after we graduated, was deeply fulfilling.

Forging a Sense of Unity

Perhaps one of the most intangible but deeply gratifying triumphs was the sense of unity we built among students. University life, with its cliques, tribal divisions, and academic rivalries, could be isolating. Throughout my leadership, I focused on fostering inclusivity and making every student feel part of a larger community. This took many forms, from organizing cross-departmental events to mediating conflicts between student groups, always working toward a common goal of a united student body.

One of the defining moments came when we organized a cultural festival celebrating Kenya's diversity. For the first time, students from every tribe, background, and department gathered in one space, sharing food, stories, and dances from their cultures. The energy was electric, and the pride on everyone's faces was undeniable. Watching the students celebrate together reminded me of the immense potential we held as a community. It was one of those rare times when I felt that we had truly achieved something lasting—a campus spirit that wasn't defined by divisions but by the beauty of our diversity.

Personal Growth and Self-Discovery

With each of these triumphs, I also experienced profound personal growth. The pressures, challenges, and responsibilities had refined me, forcing me to confront my limits and develop resilience I hadn't known I possessed. My victories weren't only public; they were deeply personal. I had learned how to be firm without being harsh, decisive without disregarding others' perspectives, and hopeful even in the face of setbacks.

Looking back, every triumph felt like a piece of a larger puzzle, each victory a part of my growth not just as a leader, but as a person. My journey had been challenging, but it was also a privilege. Each of these moments became more than just memories; they were defining milestones, reminders of the impact one could have when standing up for something bigger than oneself.

Chapter 6
Graduation and the Transition

The day of my graduation felt surreal. Four years of intense academic work, tireless campaigning, and fulfilling my leadership duties had led to this moment. Standing in line with my fellow graduates, dressed in our caps and gowns, I felt an overwhelming blend of pride, relief, and uncertainty. Everything I had worked for was about to conclude, yet I knew this was only the beginning of a new journey.

As I crossed the stage to receive my diploma, memories flooded back—those late nights studying, the vibrant campaign rallies, and the endless meetings with my team and mentors. Every struggle and every triumph had led me to this moment. I looked out into the crowd, searching for familiar faces, and spotted Professor Elyjoy Micheni, my mentor and the Director of the School of Business, smiling back at me. Her presence reminded me of the support and guidance that had been crucial to my success. She had taught me to trust my instincts, believe in my purpose, and remain steadfast even when the going got tough.

Bittersweet Goodbyes

After the ceremony, the reality of departure began to sink in. Friends who had become family were now preparing to disperse, each embarking on their unique path. Kasmuel Oure, my loyal teammate, had accepted a position with a consulting firm in Nairobi, and Adonija, with his trademark charisma, was ready to dive into the world of community organizing. James Odek, who had been a strategic mastermind during our campaign, was headed for graduate studies abroad, while Marcy Keter had secured a highly sought-after internship in the finance sector. Each goodbye was a reminder that although our time together was ending, our shared experiences and growth would keep us connected.

Letting Go of Campus Leadership

Leaving behind the student leadership roles was harder than I expected. For years, my identity had been intricately tied to serving the student body, advocating for change, and bridging divides within our campus community. Now, as I faced the reality of transitioning from a student leader to an alumnus, I felt an odd emptiness. The thrill of campaigning, the weight of representing my peers, and the satisfaction of effecting change had been deeply fulfilling. Yet, I understood that stepping away was a necessary part of growth. My work on campus had come full circle, and it was time to trust the new leaders to carry the torch forward.

Navigating the Professional World

The transition from student life to the professional world was a new kind of challenge. Armed with my experiences and my degree, I entered a competitive job market that demanded adaptability, resilience, and a willingness to learn. The skill set I had honed in leadership—conflict resolution, strategic thinking, and effective communication—served me well, but there were new dynamics to navigate. In the professional world, achievements were measured differently, and success depended on finding one's niche, proving oneself, and building credibility in an entirely new environment.

I quickly learned that leadership in the professional world took on a different shape. Here, it was less about holding a title and more about leading through example, showing initiative, and gaining trust. My previous successes provided a solid foundation, but there was an unmistakable need to continuously prove myself in this new sphere. Adapting to the demands of the professional world became a journey of humility, growth, and discovering new dimensions of my capabilities.

Staying Connected to My Purpose

As I settled into my new life beyond university, I found myself reflecting on the lessons learned during my time as a student leader. The values I had cultivated—integrity, resilience, and a commitment to service—remained at the core of my aspirations. I knew that even in this new phase, my passion for advocating for others, creating change, and uniting people around a common cause would guide me.

I stayed connected to my university community by volunteering to mentor current students, offering insights from my own experiences and hoping to inspire the next generation of leaders. I saw in them the same hunger for growth, the same passion for change, and I felt reassured that the campus community was in good hands. This involvement kept me rooted in my purpose and allowed me to give back to a community that had shaped me in so many ways.

Embracing the Journey Forward

Graduation marked both an end and a beginning. The transition wasn't without its struggles, but it was an opportunity to redefine myself, to apply what I had learned in new contexts, and to keep growing. As I moved forward, I carried with me the memories, the friendships, and the lessons that had defined my university journey. I realized that while my time as a student leader had ended, the skills, values, and purpose I had cultivated would continue to shape my path.

Looking back on my university years, I understood that leadership was more than holding a position; it was about the legacy you leave behind, the impact you have on those around you, and the values you carry forward. The transition into the next chapter of life was daunting, but I was prepared to face it, armed with the knowledge, resilience, and sense of purpose that had been forged through every struggle, every triumph, and every unforgettable moment on campus.

Preparing for Life After College

Graduating from university is exhilarating, yet it can also feel like standing on the edge of a cliff, ready to leap into the unknown. The safety net of academic life, with its familiar routines, close-knit friendships, and a clear roadmap of what to expect next, quickly fades. Life after college brings newfound independence, and with it, an urgent need to define who you are and what you want to achieve. As I approached this next chapter, I found myself both eager and anxious—ready to apply my knowledge and skills yet uncertain of where they would lead me.

Creating a Career Vision

One of my first priorities was to envision my career beyond the titles and degrees. For years, academic achievement and campus leadership had defined my path, but now I needed a broader sense of purpose. I spent time reflecting on the passions that had driven me through college a desire to uplift others, to bridge divides, and to advocate for inclusivity. These values would be the cornerstone of my career journey.

However, creating a vision meant more than simply defining what I wanted; it required understanding the "why" behind my goals. Why was I drawn to these values? And how could they manifest in a meaningful career? These questions led me to explore fields and organizations where service, leadership, and innovation intersected, expanding my perspective on the types of roles I could pursue. This process was both exciting and daunting, as I weighed options in a competitive job market.

Learning the Art of Networking

While my university network had been robust and invaluable, transitioning to the professional world required building new connections. Networking was an entirely new skill for me—one that I hadn't anticipated would play such a significant role. But the reality quickly set in connections often opened doors in ways that skills and knowledge alone could not.

At first, I was uncomfortable reaching out to strangers on professional networking platforms or attending events where I barely knew anyone. But I learned that networking wasn't just about seeking opportunities; it was about forming genuine relationships. My years in student leadership had given me the tools to communicate with people from diverse backgrounds, and I found that applying those skills in a professional setting was essential. Slowly, I built a network of mentors, peers, and industry contacts who offered not just career advice but insights that would help me grow personally and professionally.

Financial Independence and Responsibility

With graduation came a new level of financial independence—and responsibility. College had provided a buffer from certain financial realities, and I now found myself managing a budget, paying rent, and balancing the costs of living. It was eye-opening, to say the least.

To adapt, I took a step back and assessed my financial goals. I wanted to save for future educational pursuits, possibly a master's degree, and set aside funds to support my family back home. These goals were grounding, motivating me to be cautious with my spending. I became disciplined about budgeting, prioritizing needs over wants, and making sacrifices where necessary. The financial discipline I learned was invaluable, shaping my approach to long-term planning and financial security.

Personal Growth and Adaptability

College had instilled confidence and resilience, but post-graduation life tested these qualities on an entirely new level. Outside of the academic environment, there was no clear feedback system, no scheduled exams to gauge my progress. I had to seek my own validation, set my own benchmarks, and hold myself accountable for my growth.

I found comfort in reading, joining online courses, and attending workshops to continue developing skills relevant to my career. I realized that lifelong learning wasn't just a phrase; it was a practice that kept me adaptable in a rapidly changing world. I embraced this challenge, using each new experience as a chance to learn and redefine myself. It was a humbling but necessary reminder that growth doesn't end with a diploma; it is a continuous journey.

Giving Back to My Community

As I looked to the future, I was determined not to leave behind the communities that had shaped me. My experiences at university had instilled a sense of responsibility, a drive to make a difference. I volunteered to speak at youth events, sharing my experiences with students facing similar challenges, and became active in mentoring programs, helping others navigate the transitions I had faced.

Giving back was deeply fulfilling, grounding me amidst the uncertainties of post-college life. It reminded me of the purpose behind my career ambitions and kept me connected to the values that had guided me through my journey. I wanted to be a source of support for others, just as I had once been supported by Professor Elyjoy Micheni and my team members like Kasmuel Oure and Adonija.

Embracing the Unpredictable Future

With each passing day, I learned to accept that life after college wouldn't come with a predictable structure. There would be challenges, surprises, and unexpected detours. But that was part of the excitement—the freedom to explore new paths and the opportunity to redefine success on my own terms.

The journey ahead was a blank canvas, waiting to be filled with the dreams, challenges, and lessons that lay ahead. I was ready to dive in, grateful for the foundation built during my college years and eager to face whatever came next. This transition was not just a step forward; it was a leap into a world brimming with possibility.

The Reality of Graduation

Graduation was supposed to be a day of unfiltered joy, the final culmination of years of hard work and sacrifice. But when the day arrived, I found myself wrapped in a mix of emotions that I hadn't anticipated. Beneath the celebrations, the bright robes, and the countless photos lay an inescapable feeling of uncertainty—a lingering question about what came next. Walking up to receive my diploma was an accomplishment, yes, but it also felt like stepping into a new world I wasn't fully prepared for.

Facing the End of an Era

On that day, I was surrounded by my friends, mentors, and family, each of whom had been an integral part of my university journey. But as we all celebrated, I couldn't shake the feeling that an entire chapter of my life was closing. The campus, which had been like a second home, no longer felt the same. My mind flashed back to the nights spent studying for exams, the bustling campaign trails, and the countless late-night conversations with friends in the dorm. Each of those moments was tied to the unique rhythm of university life, one I realized I would never fully recapture.

Saying goodbye to the familiar hallways and crowded lecture rooms felt like saying goodbye to a part of myself. The relationships I'd built, the memories I'd made—they were irreplaceable, and the thought of leaving it all behind was bittersweet.

The Weight of Expectation

Graduation brought with it a different type of pressure. Expectations that had always felt far off were suddenly at my doorstep. Family, friends, and even my younger peers looked at me with hopeful eyes, expecting me to step seamlessly into a career and put my hard-earned degree to use. But the job market was as challenging as it was competitive, and my vision for a career was still somewhat blurry.

I wrestled with questions that seemed to have no clear answers Would I find a job that was meaningful? Would I be able to make a difference, as I had hoped to during my student leadership days? And could I live up to the high expectations that my community had for me?

The Financial Reality

Beyond the dreams and aspirations, there was the reality of finances. Graduation meant I was now responsible for managing my expenses and securing an income. Student life had provided a certain level of financial flexibility, but as a graduate, I quickly realized I'd need to adopt a more disciplined approach to money. Rent, food, transportation, and even professional attire—suddenly, the demands of daily life required a financial strategy I hadn't fully anticipated.

While I was lucky to have a strong support system, the reality of standing on my own two feet was humbling. I began looking for side gigs and applied to countless jobs, but each application and interview process felt like a balancing act between ambition and necessity.

The Gap Between Expectation and Reality

As the weeks after graduation passed, I started to understand that life after university was far more complex than I'd imagined. While student leadership had provided me with invaluable skills and experiences, it didn't fully prepared me for the unpredictability and pressures of the professional world. My classmates, too, were scattered across different paths—some pursuing further studies, others landing dream jobs, and some still searching, just like me. The stark differences in our paths brought up questions about success, timing, and the unpredictability of life.

The real world, I realized, didn't operate by the same clear-cut rules of academia or campus life. Degrees and honors didn't automatically translate to opportunities, and the process of finding one's footing was anything but straightforward.

Rediscovering Purpose

In the midst of these uncertainties, I began reflecting on the journey that had brought me this far. The leadership roles, the friendships, the mentorship from Professor Elyjoy Micheni, and the support of my team members like Kasmuel Oure, Adonija, James Odek, and Marcy Keter—they all had taught me resilience, purpose, and adaptability. These values became my anchors, reminding me that while life's path was uncertain, the foundation I'd built was strong.

I understood that the transition after graduation wasn't just about finding a job; it was about rediscovering who I was outside of the structures that had defined me for years. I took each day as an opportunity to learn, grow, and redefine success on my own terms, recognizing that this phase, too, was part of the journey.

Embracing the Journey Ahead

The reality of graduation wasn't what I'd expected, but it was exactly what I needed. It pushed me to confront the unknown, to reassess my dreams, and to accept that progress often comes in unexpected forms. The path forward wouldn't be a straight line; there would be detours, setbacks, and surprises along the way. But I was ready to face them, armed with the lessons, memories, and friendships that my university experience had given me.

And so, with a heart full of hope and a mind brimming with dreams, I took my first steps into the world beyond the university gates. Graduation had marked the end of an era, but it was also the beginning of something new—an adventure that was mine to shape, one decision, one challenge, and one triumph at a time.

Chapter 7
The Job Market Struggle

Graduation was meant to be the beginning of a bright, promising future. I had walked proudly across the stage, gripped my degree, and smiled for the cameras, fueled by the hope that I'd soon land a meaningful job and make my mark on the world. The future felt bright, as if my hard work and sacrifices were about to pay off in the form of stability, independence, and a fulfilling career. But as the excitement of graduation day faded, I quickly realized that the job market was far more unforgiving than I'd expected.

Entering the Kenyan Job Market

In Kenya, where every year sees thousands of graduates flooding an already saturated job market, the competition for meaningful work was fierce. Armed with my degree and leadership experience, I felt confident as I crafted my CV, listing every achievement and skill I had acquired. I believed that my involvement in student politics, my relationships with mentors, and my impressive academic record would give me a competitive edge.

But the reality of job hunting in Kenya was humbling, to say the least. I submitted application after application to companies across Nairobi and beyond. Days turned into weeks, then into months, as I waited to hear back. At first, there were polite rejection emails; then there was simply silence. I could feel the weight of each unanswered application, the gap between expectation and reality widening with every passing day.

The High Expectations

After graduation, my family and friends had high hopes for me. I had been a student leader, had strong grades, and a university degree that I was certain would open doors. Everyone around me assumed that I would land a good job quickly, especially with the skills and experiences I had gained on campus. Each time someone asked, "So, where are you working now?" or "Have you found anything yet?" I could feel my confidence waver. I didn't want to disappoint them, or myself, but the Kenyan job market had a way of testing even the strongest resolve.

In Kenya, many graduates find themselves taking on jobs outside their fields just to make ends meet, while others try to stay busy with unpaid internships, hoping they might eventually lead to something stable. It was difficult to reconcile my ambitions with the reality of seeing friends and peers struggling, many taking up casual jobs far from what they had studied for. I wondered if I would have to do the same.

The Hustle and Networking Culture

With each new week, I learned more about the culture of the Kenyan job market—the importance of networking, the unspoken rule that "it's not what you know, but who you know." I began reaching out to anyone I knew who could offer advice, introductions, or guidance. I attended endless networking events and industry talks, hoping to meet people who might know of job openings or even create opportunities for me. My degree and experience didn't seem to be enough on their own, but perhaps connections could fill the gaps.

Networking came with its own set of challenges. I had always thought of myself as outgoing, but the constant need to self-promote and make my case to strangers was exhausting. Some people were supportive and offered advice, while others treated me as just another job-seeking graduate in a sea of hopefuls. It was difficult not to feel lost in the crowd.

The Expense of Staying Job-Ready

Job hunting, I discovered, was an expensive endeavor. Between transportation costs to attend interviews and the price of maintaining a professional wardrobe, every bit of savings I had was dwindling fast. Each trip to Nairobi or another town for an interview or networking event felt like a gamble, especially with no guarantees of success. While I had received encouragement and words of support from my network, I was beginning to understand the financial realities of staying "ready" in a competitive job market.

For those in the middle and upper class, finding a job might have been easier, but as a new graduate, every expense added pressure. I was caught in the balance between taking any job I could find just to earn a living and holding out for something aligned with my skills and passions.

The Unexpected Turns

Just as I was beginning to feel that I might never find something in my field, a glimmer of hope appeared. I received an offer for an internship—unpaid, but in a reputable firm within my area of study. My first instinct was frustration. After years of study and leadership, was this truly all I could secure? But after much thought, I accepted. I reminded myself that sometimes, even the smallest steps can lead to larger doors.

During this internship, I worked harder than ever before, treating every day as an opportunity to prove myself. I juggled multiple side gigs to pay for transportation and meals, pushing through each week on sheer determination. While the position was temporary, it opened doors and expanded my network in ways I hadn't expected. I was reminded of the strength and resilience I had built over the years, qualities I'd gained through the struggles of student leadership and the support of my mentors like Professor Elyjoy Micheni.

Lessons in Patience and Resilience

While the transition from student leader to job seeker was not the straightforward journey I had expected, it was a lesson in patience, grit, and humility. The job market forced me to confront my assumptions about success, reminding me that even the best-prepared paths can be winding and challenging. Each setback became a lesson in resilience, each small victory a reminder of the power of persistence.

Graduation had given me a degree, but the job market gave me something equally important the drive to keep pushing forward, to embrace the process, and to hold onto my dreams even when the path was far from clear. The Kenyan job market, challenging as it was, had shown me that success wasn't just about the degree or the accolades. It was about the willingness to start again, to hustle, and to forge a path, one step at a time.

Challenges in Finding Entry-Level Positions

The thrill of graduation quickly gave way to a different reality—one marked by endless job applications and an entry-level market far more elusive than I had imagined. Armed with my degree, student leadership experience, and a head full of ambition, I stepped into the Kenyan job market expecting a clear path. However, the journey was anything but straightforward.

The Harsh Truths of "Entry-Level"

As a fresh graduate, I had always believed that "entry-level" jobs would be open to those of us just starting our careers, roles designed for recent graduate's eager to prove themselves. Instead, I was met with job postings asking for two, sometimes even three years of experience for basic roles. How was I supposed to gain experience when every "entry-level" job required it? Each job listing felt like a closed door, one that teased opportunity but stayed just out of reach.

The interviews I managed to secure were often disheartening. I walked into boardrooms and waited for hours with other candidates, each one seeming more qualified, more polished, and equally desperate to make an impression. I'd answer questions about my leadership background and my studies, but time and again, employers would return to the same point "You're impressive, but we're looking for someone with experience."

The Network Hustle

It didn't take long to realize that in Kenya, qualifications and enthusiasm were only part of the puzzle. Connections were a silent currency. I tapped into every connection I had, from old classmates to mentors, hoping someone knew of an opening, any opening, where I could get a foothold. Networking became an unspoken part of the job description—hours spent at industry events, each conversation an opportunity to secure my future.

It wasn't that I was shy or uncomfortable talking to strangers. But there's a certain exhaustion that comes from presenting yourself over and over, asking people to take a chance on you while keeping your dignity intact. It was a dance—balancing professionalism with the reality that each conversation could open a door or simply end in a polite goodbye.

The Hidden Cost of Job Hunting

Beyond the emotional toll, finding an entry-level job had a very real financial burden. Transport to and from interviews across Nairobi wasn't cheap, and professional attire added to the cost. As weeks turned into months, I began to understand how much "getting a job" required before you even secured one. Friends in similar positions often joked that the job hunt itself was a full-time job, and for many of us, it was true. Each interview that didn't yield an offer meant starting from scratch—new application, new hope, new expenses.

I had anticipated that my first job might not pay much, but I hadn't expected the waiting period to cost so much. I remember spending nights scouring online job boards, my optimism fading each time a promising role required "just a little more experience" or offered unpaid internships instead of salaried work.

Moments of Frustration and Realization

Every day without a job offer weighed on me, but one experience particularly shook me. After weeks of interviews, I was close to landing a position at a reputable company. They'd called me in multiple times, and I had even met with the department head. I felt a cautious optimism. But a few days later, I received a message saying they'd decided to go with someone with "a more extensive background."

That rejection hit differently, and it lingered. I spent days replaying every answer I'd given, wondering if I should have said something differently or highlighted my skills better. But in the end, I understood that in this competitive market, securing a job wasn't always about what I could control.

Finding Resilience in the Struggle

One night, after what felt like my hundredth application, I realized I was approaching the job hunt the same way I had tackled student politics—with grit, strategy, and patience. I reminded myself that in every setback, I had learned something valuable. The market was tough, but I wasn't powerless. I had a choice in how I responded, and I chose to keep pushing.

In time, I embraced a more strategic approach. I focused on quality over quantity in my applications, emphasizing roles that aligned with my skills and passion. I refined my resume, tailored each cover letter, and practiced my interview responses until they felt genuine. I began networking with purpose, not just for leads but to learn about the industry's demands and adjust my approach.

Finally, I received an offer—not the dream job, but an entry-level position where I could put my skills to use. It was the start I needed, a foot in the door. I accepted it with gratitude, recognizing that my journey through rejection and resilience had prepared me for this next chapter.

In Kenya's competitive job market, finding an entry-level role wasn't easy. But through the struggle, I found strength, adaptability, and a sense of purpose. This chapter may not have started the way I envisioned, but it gave me a foundation that would shape the career I was just beginning to build.

Dealing with Rejections and Setbacks

Leaving university, I felt unstoppable. With my degree and leadership experience, I was convinced the job market would welcome me with open arms. But what I found was a humbling reality, where optimism quickly turned to resilience, and resilience to sheer determination.

The First Blow

It began with my first interview at a top firm in Nairobi. I walked in confidently, answered every question with clarity, and even caught the panelists exchanging impressed glances. When I left, I was certain an offer would follow. Instead, an email arrived a few days later with a polite "We regret to inform you..." It felt like a punch. I wondered if it was my lack of job experience or a small slip-up I couldn't recall, but I couldn't escape the lingering question Was I really ready for this?

The "Almost Hired" Rollercoaster

Undeterred, I pushed forward, securing more interviews and learning from each one. Every rejection, however, seemed to sting deeper than the last. At one point, I'd been through five rounds with a company, meeting everyone from department heads to potential team members. When they told me I was their top candidate, I felt the breakthrough was here.

A week passed, then two. The "congratulations" email never came. Eventually, I got a call—a vague explanation that they'd gone with someone who "fit the team culture better." I hadn't just lost an opportunity; I felt like I'd lost time and a part of myself. Rejection was becoming less about the job and more about questioning if I was enough.

Sleepless Nights and Hard Questions

I stopped counting the number of applications I sent out. Each job had its unique promise, each rejection chipped away a little more at my confidence. Nights became a swirl of thoughts and self-doubt. I'd lie awake, replaying interviews, analyzing questions I might have answered wrong, and wondering if there was something inherently missing in me. Had I studied the wrong course? Was my leadership background even relevant?

Rejections brought up all kinds of fears. I questioned if I'd been naïve to think I could navigate the real world as easily as I had university politics. But these questions forced me to face my weaknesses head-on. I was learning to handle disappointment, understanding that it wasn't personal but part of the process.

The Turning Point A Different Approach

After months of knockbacks, I realized that endlessly applying wasn't going to work unless I changed my approach. I started seeking out mentors and connecting with people in my field who had faced similar struggles. Talking to them brought me insights beyond what any job description could offer. I learned that setbacks, while painful, could also be tools for growth. One mentor's words hit home "Every rejection is just redirection," he told me, "Don't take it as a wall; take it as a guide."

Inspired, I honed my applications, focusing on positions where I could highlight my unique strengths, particularly my experience in student leadership and my capacity to solve complex problems under pressure. I began targeting companies where my skills would shine, rather than merely matching a list of qualifications. Rejections still came, but I was gaining ground in ways that mattered.

The Call I Wasn't Expecting

One Tuesday afternoon, after a particularly disappointing morning interview, my phone buzzed. It was from a company I'd barely remembered applying to. "We'd like to offer you a position," they said. I sat in stunned silence. After months of setbacks, the relief felt surreal. It wasn't my dream job, but it was a start—a place where I could learn and grow.

Rejection as Redirection

As I prepared to step into this role, I understood that the rejection and setbacks had not been a waste. They had sharpened my resilience and forced me to uncover strengths I hadn't known I possessed. Rejection had shown me the reality of the job market, but it had also taught me that each "no" was nudging me toward a "yes"—just in a way I hadn't expected.

In the end, my story wasn't just about landing a job. It was about finding my footing, growing in confidence, and learning that setbacks don't define you; they refine you. Each rejection had been a lesson, and through that hard path, I had discovered something invaluable my own resilience.

Chapter 8
Fitting into Corporate Culture

Stepping into the world of corporate Kenya as a salesperson in a reputable bank was nothing short of a culture shock. I had walked into that office armed with the courage and boldness honed during my years in university. The countless debates, leadership challenges, and social interactions on campus had made me outspoken, confident, and assertive. But what had been celebrated in the university context quickly became a double-edged sword in the corporate environment.

Adjusting to the Corporate Environment

The first weeks were a whirlwind of frustration and loneliness. I was eager to make an impression, but my boldness was met with raised eyebrows and whispered judgments. I questioned practices I didn't understand, offered unsolicited ideas in meetings, and didn't shy away from engaging with senior colleagues. To me, it was natural to seek clarity and challenge the norm; to them, it was presumptuous and disrespectful.

The corporate hierarchy was something I hadn't fully grasped. Unlike the university setting where student leaders and peers were treated with mutual respect, the bank had unspoken rules about how to interact with superiors. Here, juniors were expected to listen more than they spoke, follow before they led, and nod in agreement even when they disagreed. My audacity didn't fit the mold, and my colleagues and superiors made no effort to hide their displeasure.

It wasn't just the professional dynamics that felt alienating. My colleagues often bonded over shared experiences and inside jokes, leaving me feeling like an outsider. Office lunches, group chats, and after-work drinks became dreaded events as I struggled to find common ground. The sense of isolation was suffocating.

The culmination of my struggle came during a department review meeting. I had been assigned a task to analyze customer feedback, and I presented my findings with confidence, even pointing out gaps in the team's approach. Instead of recognition, I was met with stony silence and passive-aggressive comments afterward. The words "too much" and "overstepping" floated back to me through whispers. For the first time, I questioned whether I truly belonged in this world.

Overcoming Gender Stereotypes

Being a young woman in banking came with its unique set of challenges. While the field boasted many accomplished women, the underlying stereotypes persisted. I felt the weight of expectations to be agreeable, reserved, and pliable. My assertiveness was frequently misinterpreted as arrogance, and my straightforwardness was deemed "unfeminine."

One incident, in particular, stayed with me. A male colleague openly commented during a team meeting, "You're too aggressive for someone just starting out." It wasn't the words that stung the most—it was the murmurs of agreement from others in the room. That day, I resolved to tone myself down, to mold myself into the version of a corporate employee they seemed to want. But even as I tried, the discomfort of suppressing my true self weighed heavily on me.

It was during these difficult days that I met Madam Anne Mucira. She was the Bank Operations Manager, and she quickly became my guiding light in what had felt like an endless tunnel of darkness.

Building Professional Relationships Madam Anne's Mentorship

Madam Anne was a striking figure—graceful yet commanding, warm yet firm. She had an air of authority that didn't need to be announced. She noticed me during one of the branch's weekly meetings, where I had been uncharacteristically quiet. After the session, she called me to her office.

"How are you finding it here?" she asked gently, her tone disarming. For the first time, someone wasn't interrogating me but genuinely inquiring about my experience. The floodgates opened. I spoke about my struggles, my isolation, and how I felt misunderstood. She listened intently, her eyes full of understanding.

"You're bold," she finally said, a smile tugging at her lips. "And that's a good thing. But boldness without finesse can be misinterpreted. Let me show you how to navigate this space without losing who you are."

From that day, Madam Anne became my mentor, and in many ways, a second mother. She taught me the nuances of corporate etiquette, from how to frame my opinions tactfully to the power of listening more than I spoke. She showed me how to build alliances subtly, by supporting colleagues and letting my work speak for itself.

She didn't just mentor me professionally—she took me under her wing personally. She invited me to her home for lunch on weekends, introduced me to her family, and shared stories of her own struggles as a young woman in the banking sector. Her journey was a mirror of my own, and her resilience became my inspiration.

"Don't let them dim your light," she often told me. "But learn to adjust its intensity to suit the room."

Under her guidance, I began to thrive. I learned how to present my ideas in ways that didn't come across as confrontational. I built rapport with colleagues by finding shared interests and offering to help on tasks. Slowly, the walls around me started to crumble, and the relationships I had struggled to forge began to form naturally.

The Transformation

Fitting into corporate culture didn't mean losing myself—it meant learning how to adapt without compromising my core values. Madam Anne taught me that navigating the corporate world was as much about emotional intelligence as it was about competence.

By the end of my first year at the bank, I was no longer the misunderstood, isolated rookie. I had built meaningful relationships, earned the respect of my colleagues, and, most importantly, found my place in the corporate ecosystem.

Looking back, I realized that my struggles had been necessary stepping stones. They had forced me to grow, to adapt, and to become resilient. Madam Anne's mentorship wasn't just about surviving in the corporate world—it was about thriving in it while staying true to myself.

Chapter 9
Personal Growth and Resilience

Personal growth is rarely a smooth, upward climb; it's a journey marked by stumbles, recalibrations, and moments of revelation. As I ventured from the familiar confines of university life into the uncharted waters of adulthood and corporate Kenya, I found myself on a path of profound self-discovery. It was a journey fueled by struggles, punctuated by triumphs, and ultimately defined by resilience.

Lessons Learned from Struggles

My entry into the professional world was humbling. I quickly discovered that the audacity and boldness that had propelled me to success in university leadership did not always translate well into corporate spaces. Instead of being celebrated, my forthrightness was met with suspicion and sometimes hostility. The confident young leader was suddenly navigating an environment where I was viewed as "too much" or "too difficult."

It was a bitter pill to swallow. I had to confront the fact that I was an outsider in a system with its own unwritten rules. My struggles weren't limited to perception alone; they extended to the lack of resources, institutional bureaucracy, and my own insecurities about whether I was truly cut out for this world.

One incident stands out vividly in my memory. During a departmental meeting, I raised a question about a process that seemed inefficient. It was a genuine inquiry, driven by curiosity and a desire to improve. But the room fell silent, and the glances exchanged between my colleagues spoke volumes. Later, a senior colleague pulled me aside and said, "You need to learn how to choose your battles. Some questions are better left unasked."

At first, her comment stung. I felt dismissed, misunderstood, and even a little ashamed. But upon reflection, I realized that she wasn't entirely wrong. Corporate spaces required not just boldness but also strategy. I had to learn how to navigate these dynamics without compromising who I was.

From these struggles, I gained a deeper understanding of patience and humility. I learned to listen more than I spoke, to observe before I acted, and to approach challenges with a quiet resolve. These were lessons forged in the fire of adversity, lessons I carried with me long after the wounds they left had healed.

Developing Confidence and Skills

If my struggles taught me patience, my victories—however small—taught me confidence. But confidence doesn't appear magically; it's cultivated through effort, preparation, and perseverance.

One turning point came when I was asked to lead a client presentation after my supervisor called in sick. It was a high-stakes moment for someone at my level, and I was terrified. But I knew this was my chance to prove myself. I prepared obsessively, staying up late to ensure I had every detail covered.

When the day arrived, my palms were sweaty, and my heart raced as I stood in front of the room. But as I began to speak, something shifted. The hours of preparation kicked in, and I found my rhythm. I explained our proposal with clarity and conviction, fielded questions confidently, and, to my surprise, received nods of approval from the client.

That experience became a cornerstone of my growing confidence. It reminded me that preparation was my superpower. I didn't have to be the smartest or most experienced person in the room; I just needed to be the most prepared.

Over time, I also developed a repertoire of skills that set me apart. I honed my ability to communicate effectively, even in tense situations. I learned to write concise yet impactful emails, give presentations that resonated, and build consensus among diverse teams. I became adept at time management, juggling deadlines and tasks without losing focus.

But perhaps the most valuable skill I developed was adaptability. Corporate culture is ever-changing, and success often depends on your ability to pivot when circumstances demand it. I learned to embrace change, to see it not as a threat but as an opportunity to innovate and grow.

Importance of Networking and Mentorship

If there's one truth about succeeding in the corporate world, it's this no one makes it alone. Networking and mentorship became the twin pillars of my professional growth.

At first, networking felt unnatural to me. The idea of attending events, shaking hands, and exchanging pleasantries seemed superficial. But I soon realized that networking wasn't about collecting business cards—it was about building genuine connections.

One of the most impactful networking moments came during a staff team-building retreat. I struck up a conversation with a senior manager who shared insights about her own career journey. That casual conversation led to her becoming an advocate for me within the organization, recommending me for projects and encouraging my growth.

Mentorship, however, was the real game-changer. Meeting Madam Anne Mucira was nothing short of serendipitous. As the bank's operations manager, she was a force to be reckoned with—efficient, respected, and deeply empathetic. But what set her apart was her motherly demeanor. She took me under her wing, not just as a mentee but almost as a daughter.

Anne's mentorship went beyond professional advice. She taught me how to navigate office politics, how to present myself in meetings, and even how to dress for different corporate occasions. But more than that, she helped me regain my sense of self.

During one particularly difficult period when I felt ostracized by some colleagues, Anne invited me to lunch and said something I'll never forget "Don't let them dim your light. Your boldness is your gift. But like any gift, you have to learn when and how to use it."

Her words were a turning point for me. I stopped trying to fit into a mold that wasn't meant for me and started embracing my unique strengths. I learned how to be bold without being abrasive, assertive without being dismissive.

Through Anne, I also realized the importance of mentorship as a reciprocal relationship. As I grew in my role, I began mentoring younger colleagues, sharing the lessons I had learned and encouraging them to find their own path.

The Transformative Power of Resilience

Personal growth isn't about avoiding challenges; it's about transforming them into stepping stones. My journey taught me that resilience isn't a trait you're born with—it's a skill you develop through practice.

With each struggle, I became stronger. With each setback, I learned to adapt. And with each victory, I gained the confidence to dream bigger. My growth wasn't just about surviving corporate life; it was about thriving in it.

As I reflect on those early days, I realize how much I owe to the struggles I faced, the mentors who guided me, and the inner strength I discovered along the way. The journey wasn't easy, but it was worth it. I emerged not just as a better professional but as a better person—one who understood the value of perseverance, the power of connection, and the limitless potential within.

Chapter 10
Moving Forward

The end of one chapter is often the beginning of another. My journey through university leadership, the struggles of entering the corporate world, and the lessons learned along the way had shaped me into someone far removed from the young, idealistic student who first stepped onto campus grounds. Yet, in many ways, I still carried that idealism within me—now tempered with experience, resilience, and a deeper understanding of what it takes to thrive in a complex world.

Embracing Continuous Growth

By this point, I had come to accept that growth is never truly complete. It's a constant process of learning, unlearning, and relearning. The challenges I faced as a student leader, the hurdles of finding my footing in the job market, and the tough lessons in corporate culture had instilled in me a hunger for self-improvement.

I enrolled in professional development courses, attended workshops, and even began reading voraciously on topics like leadership, emotional intelligence, and personal branding. I sought out opportunities to expand my skill set, understanding that in a competitive job market, standing still was not an option.

One significant step forward was enrolling in a certified program in financial analysis—a field I had grown increasingly interested in during my banking days. It was an intense journey, juggling work and studies, but it was also deeply fulfilling. The more I invested in myself, the clearer my vision for the future became.

Paying It Forward

If there was one recurring theme in my life, it was the impact of mentorship and community. From Professor Elyjoy Micheni's wisdom during my university years to Madam Anne Mucira's guidance in the corporate world, I had been shaped by people who believed in me even when I struggled to believe in myself.

Now, it was my turn to pay it forward. I began mentoring young professionals who were just starting their careers, particularly women navigating male-dominated industries. It wasn't just about giving back; it was about creating a ripple effect. If I could help one person overcome the hurdles I had faced, they, in turn, could help others.

I also became more involved in community initiatives. Whether it was speaking at youth empowerment forums or volunteering in mentorship programs for high school students, I found immense joy in sharing my journey and inspiring others to chase their dreams fearlessly.

Redefining Success

For a long time, I equated success with titles, accolades, and material achievements. But as I progressed in my career and reflected on my journey, I realized that true success was far more personal. It was about growth, impact, and authenticity.

I stopped measuring myself against others and started focusing on my own path. Success became about finding fulfillment in my work, building meaningful relationships, and staying true to my values. It was a liberating shift, one that allowed me to find joy in the journey rather than being consumed by the destination.

Charting New Horizons

As I looked ahead, I knew there were still mountains to climb. I dreamed of one day starting my own venture, perhaps in financial consulting or leadership training, leveraging my experiences to create a platform that empowered others.

But for now, I was content to take things one step at a time. Life had taught me the value of patience and the importance of trusting the process. Each challenge I faced had prepared me for the next, and I was confident that whatever lay ahead, I had the tools to navigate it.

A Journey Worth Telling

Moving forward wasn't just about career goals or personal milestones—it was about embracing the story I was writing. Every struggle, every triumph, every lesson learned was a chapter in a narrative that was uniquely mine.

As I stood at the intersection of past, present, and future, I felt a deep sense of gratitude. Gratitude for the people who had lifted me up, for the challenges that had strengthened me, and for the journey that had brought me to this point.

The road ahead was uncertain, but it was also full of possibility. And as I moved forward, I carried with me the lessons of the past, the courage of the present, and the dreams of the future—a testament to the resilience, growth, and boundless potential that lay within us all.

Current Endeavors and Future Goals

The day I stepped out of my corporate office for the final time, I wasn't just leaving a job—I was stepping into a new chapter of my life. The years of navigating university leadership, enduring the tumult of the job market, and climbing the corporate ladder had taught me invaluable lessons. But as the elevator doors closed behind me, I knew it was time to bet on myself. The faint vision I had carried for years was about to come to life *Finsmart Hub*.

Current Endeavors Building the Foundation

Finsmart Hub wasn't born out of a eureka moment but from years of observing an unmet need in Kenya's entrepreneurial landscape. Too often, I saw brilliant minds with transformative ideas struggle to sustain their ventures—not for lack of passion but due to limited access to financial knowledge and tools.

I started small, hosting financial literacy workshops in community halls, where budding entrepreneurs could openly share their challenges. These intimate sessions taught foundational skills like budgeting, managing cash flow, and pitching to investors. Seeing attendees' eyes light up as they grasped complex concepts reaffirmed my purpose.

Empowering Marginalized Groups

My passion extended to empowering marginalized groups, especially women and youth, who often faced systemic barriers in accessing capital and mentorship. Collaborating with NGOs, I helped launch initiatives to provide financial literacy programs and sustainability training. These were not just workshops—they were spaces for transformation. I watched timid participants evolve into confident, capable individuals ready to seize opportunities.

Through these efforts, *Finsmart Hub* became more than a resource; it became a community. Each success story, no matter how small, fueled my belief that this was only the beginning.

Mentorship and Advocacy

Understanding the power of mentorship from my own journey, I became deeply committed to guiding others. Whether it was offering practical advice or simply being a listening ear, I poured my energy into creating mentorship structures through *Finsmart Hub*.

Beyond financial education, I began advocating for systemic changes to make entrepreneurship more inclusive. I envisioned a world where young entrepreneurs wouldn't have to navigate the struggles I did alone.

Future Goals Dreaming Big, Moving Boldly

While *Finsmart Hub* had taken off, my vision for its future remained expansive.

Scaling the Platform

My dream was to transform *Finsmart Hub* into a global leader in financial education and entrepreneurial support. I wanted to leverage technology to scale its reach, creating digital courses and tools accessible across Kenya and beyond. These resources would provide practical lessons on everything from financial management to market strategy, ensuring that anyone with an internet connection could benefit.

A Social Enterprise with Impact

I aspired to incorporate a microfinance arm into *Finsmart Hub*. This initiative would offer small loans to entrepreneurs who lacked traditional access to credit. More importantly, it would teach recipients how to manage debt responsibly, ensuring long-term sustainability for their businesses.

In addition, I envisioned a mentorship pipeline where successful entrepreneurs could guide newcomers through their journeys. This would foster a pay-it-forward culture, creating a ripple effect of support and success.

Global Advocacy and Thought Leadership

Locally rooted but globally minded, I aimed to position *Finsmart Hub* as a thought leader in financial inclusion and entrepreneurship. By contributing to research, publishing articles, and speaking at conferences, I hoped to influence policies and spark conversations about how small businesses could drive sustainable development in Africa.

Balancing Ambition with Action

Despite my grand vision, I understood that progress required patience. Each workshop I facilitated, every entrepreneur I mentored, and every partnership I cultivated was a building block toward this future.

There were challenges—days when doubt crept in and resources felt limited. But my journey had taught me resilience. I knew that meaningful change wasn't instantaneous; it was the result of consistent effort, adaptability, and an unyielding belief in the mission.

A Legacy of Purpose

Reflecting on my journey, I saw how every chapter of my life had prepared me for this moment. University leadership taught me the value of community and persistence. The corporate world sharpened my skills and discipline. And the challenges I faced along the way built my character.

Finsmart Hub wasn't just a career move—it was a culmination of everything I believed in. It was about more than financial literacy or entrepreneurship. It was about creating opportunities, instilling confidence, and paving a way for others to follow.

As I looked ahead, I knew the road wouldn't be easy. But for the first time, I wasn't just walking a path—I was building it. And that made every challenge, every step, and every dream worth it.

The story of *Finsmart Hub* was my story, but it was also the story of countless dreamers and changemakers who refused to settle. Together, we were proving that with the right tools, resilience, and community, anything was possible.

And the best part? This journey was just beginning.

Continuing to Advocate for Women in Leadership

The journey of leadership is never truly complete, especially for women in Kenya, where barriers persist despite progress. My experiences as a university leader, a corporate professional, and now the founder of Finsmart Hub have reinforced my commitment to championing women in leadership roles. It's a mission deeply personal to me—one shaped by the battles I've fought and the mentors who guided me.

Breaking the Glass Ceiling

The struggles I faced as a young woman leader taught me that gender often complicates the leadership journey. From stereotypes to outright discrimination, I witnessed firsthand the biases that hold women back. In university, I had to fight for my voice to be heard; in the corporate world, my assertiveness was misinterpreted as arrogance. These challenges were not unique to me—they are the reality for many women navigating leadership spaces in Kenya and beyond.

Through Finsmart Hub, I've made it a priority to support women entrepreneurs and leaders. Whether through financial literacy workshops or mentorship programs, I aim to create spaces where women can learn, grow, and thrive without fear of judgment.

Mentorship Paying It Forward

Reflecting on my own journey, I remember how Professor Elyjoy Micheni shaped my confidence as a student leader and how Madam Anne Mucira helped me navigate the corporate maze. These women showed me the transformative power of mentorship, and I've made it my mission to pay that forward.

At Finsmart Hub, I've established a mentorship initiative specifically for women. We pair young leaders with seasoned professionals who understand the unique challenges women face in leadership. These relationships are designed to not only build skills but also instill the confidence needed to break societal molds.

One of our most impactful programs is EmpowerHer Talks, a monthly series where women leaders from various sectors share their journeys, struggles, and triumphs. These conversations foster a sense of community and inspire the next generation of women to aim higher.

Creating Systemic Change

While mentorship and education are critical, I believe in tackling systemic issues head-on. Advocacy plays a significant role in my work. I've been part of panels, forums, and policymaking discussions, pushing for better representation of women in leadership.

From advocating for maternity-friendly policies in workplaces to lobbying for increased funding for women-led businesses, I've made it my mission to address the structural barriers that hinder women's advancement.

In partnership with NGOs and government agencies, Finsmart Hub has also launched initiatives aimed at increasing access to capital for women entrepreneurs. These programs are designed to close the funding gap that disproportionately affects women, empowering them to start and scale their businesses.

Inspiring a New Generation

One of my greatest joys is working with young women who aspire to lead. In our workshops, I often share my own story—not just the successes but the struggles, too. I tell them about the moments of doubt, the rejections, and the resilience it took to keep moving forward.

Seeing these women embrace their potential reminds me why this work matters. Leadership is not just about breaking barriers for oneself; it's about ensuring that the next generation doesn't have to face the same obstacles.

Future Goals for Advocacy

Looking ahead, I'm determined to expand these efforts. My vision is to create a Women in Leadership Institute under the Finsmart Hub umbrella. This institute will provide leadership training, mentorship, and advocacy resources for women across Kenya.

The goal is to not only prepare women for leadership roles but to reshape the narrative around women in power. I want to see a Kenya where women leaders are celebrated for their competence and vision rather than scrutinized for their gender.

A Lifelong Commitment

Advocating for women in leadership is more than a career goal; it's a lifelong mission. I'm deeply aware that the strides we make today will shape the opportunities available tomorrow.

For every woman who steps into a boardroom, runs for office, or starts her own business, the impact ripples far beyond her immediate circle. It changes perceptions, challenges biases, and opens doors for countless others.

As I continue this journey, I hold onto the belief that leadership isn't about standing out—it's about lifting others up. Together, we can create a future where women's voices are not just heard but amplified, and their leadership isn't the exception but the norm.

Inspiring the Next Generation of Leaders

From the moment I hosted my first workshop, I realized that empowering others wasn't just an ambition; it was my calling. Each session was a journey of transformation—both for the participants and for me. Through entrepreneurship training, financial literacy education, and support for budding entrepreneurs, I found a platform to impart the knowledge and experiences that had shaped my own path.

My goal was clear to create a generation of leaders who weren't just business-savvy but also socially conscious and resilient. Whether it was teaching budgeting basics to young entrepreneurs or guiding established small business owners on accessing markets and pitching to investors, the work became deeply fulfilling.

The Role of Mentorship Irene Odongo's Impact

While I had the vision for Finsmart Hub, its true shape and potential were brought into focus with the help of Irene Odongo. Irene, a seasoned entrepreneur and mentor, came into my life like a steady lighthouse during a storm. Her wisdom and practical advice were invaluable as I navigated the complexities of building a sustainable platform.

Irene had a unique way of balancing tough love with encouragement. "Dream big, but make your plans bigger," she once told me during one of our many brainstorming sessions. She helped me streamline my ideas, focus on achievable goals, and envision Finsmart Hub as more than just a local initiative—it could become a global force for good.

Her mentorship didn't just shape the strategy; it also molded me. Irene taught me to lead with both empathy and precision, reminding me that building people was just as important as building a business.

Building the Leaders of Tomorrow

The workshops evolved into more than just training sessions. They became incubators of innovation, where entrepreneurs—young and old—could connect, learn, and grow. Every question asked, every struggle shared, was a testament to the hunger for growth and the need for guidance.

To inspire the next generation, I've incorporated mentorship pipelines into Finsmart Hub. Irene's influence inspired me to ensure that every entrepreneur who joins our programs is paired with a mentor who can guide them through the challenges of starting and sustaining a business.

My belief is simple leaders aren't born; they are built. And it's through shared wisdom, collaboration, and resilience that we can mold a brighter future. Every person who walks into a Finsmart workshop walks out with not just knowledge but the belief that they can create meaningful change.

Continuing the Legacy

Through this work, I see my own legacy unfolding—not as an individual success story but as a collective one. By empowering others, I am building a ripple effect of impact. Irene's mentorship reminds me that leadership is not about being at the top; it's about lifting others as you climb.

As I continue to inspire the next generation of leaders, my hope is that they will do the same for those who come after them. It's a cycle of empowerment, and it's only just beginning.

Chapter 11
Reflection on the Journey

As I look back on the long and winding path that has brought me here, the reflection is not just on the highs and the triumphs, but also on the lessons learned from the struggles, the setbacks, and the people who shaped me along the way.

From my early days as a student leader to stepping out of the corporate world to pursue my own vision with Finsmart Hub, it has been a journey marked by growth, resilience, and an unwavering belief in the power of leadership. The experiences, the challenges, and the victories have all contributed to who I am today.

Throughout this journey, I have been guided by many mentors, friends, and supporters—people who believed in me when I couldn't believe in myself. They have pushed me, shaped my vision, and helped me grow. But none of this would have been possible without the foundation laid by my family. My father, the late Joram Lwambe Okola, was the first person to show me what true leadership meant. He mentored me into understanding the responsibilities that come with leadership from a young age. His wisdom and lessons continue to resonate with me, even in his absence.

My mother, Sabina Okola, has been a constant source of strength, a pillar of hope when things felt impossible. Her unwavering belief in me has kept me going, especially during the toughest moments. My sibling, Eric Okola, has also been a guiding light, always there with life advice and encouragement. My other siblings have been my steadfast supporters, always cheering me on, offering their help, and reminding me that I wasn't alone in this journey.

The path to leadership wasn't a straight line; it was a series of moments where courage collided with fear, where doubt mixed with determination. From my days as a class representative to running for vice president, to navigating the corporate world, and finally stepping into entrepreneurship through Finsmart Hub, every chapter of this journey has taught me something invaluable.

There were moments when I questioned if I was on the right path. When rejections and setbacks felt like walls I couldn't climb. When the expectations placed on me as a woman leader seemed heavier than I could bear. But in those moments, I learned something essential growth happens when we push through the discomfort, when we confront our fears, and when we refuse to let challenges define us.

What I've come to realize is that leadership is not about a title, a position, or a moment of recognition—it's about the journey itself, the process of becoming who you are meant to be, and how you show up for others along the way. Leadership is about being of service, making a difference, and lifting others as you rise. The obstacles I faced only made me stronger, more resilient, and more committed to my purpose. Every setback was a lesson in disguise, and every victory, no matter how small, was a testament to the power of perseverance.

Final Thoughts on Leadership and Growth

Leadership, at its core, is a journey of continuous growth. It's not defined by titles or positions but by the willingness to evolve, to learn from both success and failure, and to inspire those around you. Over the years, I've come to understand that growth isn't always about making giant leaps forward—sometimes it's the small, consistent steps that shape us into the leaders we aspire to be.

I've learned that true leadership is about self-awareness—knowing your strengths and, equally, understanding your weaknesses. It's about being humble enough to admit when you don't have all the answers and strong enough to seek them. The best leaders are those who aren't afraid to grow, adapt, and, most importantly, listen. Leadership is as much about serving others as it is about guiding them, and that means being willing to change your approach when something isn't working.

The path to leadership is also paved with resilience. I've seen firsthand how challenges, disappointments, and even failures, when embraced with the right mindset, are often the best teachers. Leadership isn't about avoiding setbacks—it's about how you rise when they happen. Every time I encountered an obstacle, I had to remind myself that this was just part of the journey, not the end. Growth comes from navigating the difficult times and learning to adapt, stay focused, and remain true to your vision.

One of the most powerful lessons I've learned is that growth isn't always a solo endeavor. It happens in community, in relationships, and in the mentorships we build along the way. Having mentors like Irene Odongo, who shaped the vision for Finsmart Hub, or learning from other leaders who have walked this path before me, has shown me that leadership is not something you do alone. It's about lifting others up, sharing wisdom, and creating an environment where everyone can succeed. It's a cycle of growth that continuously feeds itself.

True leadership is also about impact—the kind of difference you make in the lives of others. It's easy to get caught up in personal success, but I've realized that the greatest fulfillment comes from helping others succeed, too. As I reflect on my own journey, I see that every step I took, every initiative I launched, was not just about building my own career—it was about creating opportunities for others, especially in entrepreneurship and financial literacy. Leadership is about leaving a legacy, about making sure that the work you do ripples out, empowering others to rise to their own potential.

In all of this, I've come to understand that growth is a choice—a commitment to push through the tough times, to continually challenge yourself, and to never stop learning. It's about taking the lessons from the past and using them to fuel your future.

As I continue my journey in entrepreneurship, leadership, and advocacy, I am reminded that growth is not an end state but a lifelong process. And while I've come a long way, I know there is still so much more to learn, achieve, and contribute.

Leadership is about embracing that journey fully, with all its ups and downs, and using it to make a lasting impact. So, as I look ahead, I do so with the confidence that the growth and lessons I've experienced will only continue to shape the leader I strive to be—one who lifts others, creates change, and continues to grow along the way.

Encouragement for Readers

To every reader who has taken this journey with me—whether you are at the beginning of your own path or already deep in your leadership journey—I want to leave you with a simple truth you are capable of more than you think.

I know there are moments in life when doubt creeps in, when the road ahead seems uncertain, and when the weight of your ambitions feels heavier than you can carry. I've been there. I've faced rejections, obstacles, and times when I questioned whether I was on the right path. But in those moments, I also learned something invaluable growth doesn't happen in comfort zones. It happens when we dare to step into the unknown, when we push through the fear, and when we trust ourselves to navigate the challenges.

If you're standing at the crossroads of decision, uncertain whether to take that leap, I encourage you to move forward with courage. Leadership is not a destination; it's a journey.

It's about making choices that align with your values, being bold enough to embrace change, and being open to learning—whether from success or failure. There will always be obstacles, but the true measure of leadership is not in how many times you fall, but in how many times you rise and keep moving forward.

Don't be afraid to dream big. The world is waiting for your ideas, your leadership, and your unique contribution. The challenges you face today are only stepping stones to the future you are building. Whether it's entrepreneurship, climbing the corporate ladder, or stepping into any other area of leadership, know that the skills, resilience, and wisdom you develop along the way will shape you into the leader you're meant to become.

And remember, you don't have to do it alone. Surround yourself with people who believe in you, who challenge you, and who help you grow. Find mentors who will guide you, peers who will walk with you, and those who will inspire you to keep moving forward when the journey feels tough.

Leadership isn't about perfection—it's about progress. Embrace the process, trust your vision, and always be true to yourself. Keep pushing forward, even when things get tough. Your story is still unfolding, and the best chapters are yet to come.

You've got this.

Keep believing in your potential. Keep striving for growth. And above all, keep leading with purpose.

Appendix

The appendix is where additional resources, acknowledgments, and supplementary information related to the journey shared in this book are provided. Here, I will share key moments, lessons, and tools that helped shape my experience. These insights are meant to support you as you continue your own journey.

Resources for Aspiring Leaders and Entrepreneurs

Throughout my journey, I have come across various resources that helped me grow as a leader and entrepreneur. Here are a few tools and books that have been influential in shaping my leadership philosophy and entrepreneurial mindset

Books on Leadership and Growth

The 21 Irrefutable Laws of Leadership by John C. Maxwell

Start with Why by Simon Sinek

Dare to Lead by Brené Brown

The Lean Startup by Eric Ries

Financial Literacy Resources

Rich Dad Poor Dad by Robert Kiyosaki

The Total Money Makeover by Dave Ramsey

Online courses on financial management and budgeting (available on platforms like Coursera, Udemy, and LinkedIn Learning)

Entrepreneurship Development

The Hard Thing About Hard Things by Ben Horowitz

Zero to One by Peter Thiel

*Local entrepreneurship incubators and networks such as **Nailab** and **The iHub** in Nairobi, which provide mentorship, funding opportunities, and resources for entrepreneurs.*

Networking and Mentorship

***LinkedIn** Building an online presence and connecting with industry professionals has opened countless doors.*

***Mentorship Programs** Look for local mentorship programs within universities, business associations, and NGOs focused on entrepreneurship and women's leadership.*

Additional Learnings and Key Takeaways

1. **Leadership is a Journey, Not a Destination**. There is no perfect leader, and no matter how much you grow, there is always something to learn. Embrace the process and the lessons along the way.
2. **Resilience is Key**. There will be days filled with

doubt, setbacks, and challenges. But resilience is what allows you to keep moving forward, learning, and adapting.

3. **Building Relationships is Crucial** As an entrepreneur and leader, the connections you build—whether with mentors, peers, or team members—will be the foundation of your success. Never underestimate the power of a strong network.

4. **Purpose Drives Success** Know why you're doing what you're doing. Having a clear sense of purpose and vision will help you navigate challenges and keep you motivated during tough times.

Contact Information

For more information on **Finsmart Hub**, mentorship opportunities, financial literacy workshops, and entrepreneurship training, you can reach out through the following platforms

Website www.finsmarthub.com[1]

Email info@finsmarthub.com

Social Media

Facebook @FinsmartHub[2]

Instagram @FinsmartHub[3]

---

1. http://www.finsmarthub.com

2. https://facebook.com/FinsmartHub

3. https://instagram.com/FinsmartHub

Twitter @FinsmartHub[4]

Final Word

As you move forward in your own life, leadership, and entrepreneurial journey, remember that every challenge is an opportunity in disguise, every failure is a lesson, and every step forward—no matter how small—is progress. My journey is a testament to the power of persistence, vision, and community.

May you continue to dream big, lead with purpose, and empower those around you.

---

4. https://twitter.com/FinsmartHub

www.ingramcontent.com/pod-product-compliance
Lightning Source LLC
Chambersburg PA
CBHW072011150726
47999CB00002B/604